UNI DIRECTIONAL TRADE STRATEGIES©

UDTS©
Intraday Trading

UDTS ©

Boon for Intraday Traders

Stock Trading is a game of probability not luck. Trader can be a winner by understanding Demand, Supply and Trend Analysis only. UDTS© is the perfect way to understand all 3 factors together with certain rules, thus helping trader to reach to a precise conclusion and gives them highest probability to win.

Summarising UDTS®- The Strategy for a common man to trade with confidence

1. UDTS® is a unique strategy for simple and smart trading.
2. It is a copyright programme of IFMC®.
3. UDTS® is a boon for Stock Market traders and investors.
4. The strategies have made stock trading very simple for the common man.
5. No cumbersome tools of Technical Analysis are used in this strategy.
6. UDTS® is the best mechanism for emotionless trading.
7. UDTS® is a bunch of nine intraday and positional trading strategies and can be used in all segments like capital, F&O, commodity, and currency markets.
8. UDTS® is based on principles of demand and supply behaviours.
9. UDTS® is liked globally and is catching the eyes of traders and investors for its simplicity, accuracy, and higher probability of winning in stock trading.
10. Not only in India, strategy is famous in over 170+ countries worldwide.

UNI DIRECTIONAL TRADE STRATEGIES©

UDTS

Intraday Trading

The Ultimate Weapon to Become a Professional Trader

A comprehensive guide for beginners and intraday traders to learn simple trading strategies and make the right decisions at the right time

(Based on the author's personal and practical trading experience)

Manish Taneja

SENIOR RESEARCH ANALYST IFMC®

www.whitefalconpublishing.com

UDTS© - Intraday Trading Brahmastra
Manish Taneja

www.whitefalconpublishing.com

All rights reserved
First Edition, 2023
© Manish Taneja, 2023
Cover design by Manish Taneja, 2023

No part of this publication may be reproduced, or stored in a retrieval system, or transmitted in any form by means of electronic, mechanical, photocopying or otherwise, without prior written permission from the publisher.

The contents of this book have been certified and timestamped on the Gnosis blockchain as a permanent proof of existence.
Scan the QR code or visit the URL given on the back cover to verify the blockchain certification for this book.

The views expressed in this work are solely those of the author and do not reflect the views of the publisher, and the publisher hereby disclaims any responsibility for them.

Requests for permission should be addressed to the publisher.

ISBN - 978-1-63640-825-5

Manish Taneja

"Stock Market Is Easy When You Know How."

DISCLAIMER OF WARRANTIES AND LIMITATION OF LIABILITY

The handbook's content is drafted solely for informational purposes only to aid the traders in making their own trading decisions. The information contained herein is based on the author's knowledge, experience, and expertise. The book is not intended to be used as the primary basis for trading decisions, nor is it intended as a recommendation to buy or sell any security.

A word of caution: traders must understand the statistics involved in the stock market and correlate the information to make informed decisions about which stocks to buy and sell.

We (The author and Publisher) make no representations or warranties of any kind, express or implied, about the completeness, accuracy, reliability, suitability, or availability of the handbook or the information, products, services, or related graphics contained in the book for any purpose. We shall not be liable for any loss or profit or any other commercial damages, whether special, incidental, or consequential, for the decisions the readers made based on the information given in the book.

We strongly recommend that readers go through IFMC®'s online course on Uni-Directional Trade Strategies© for better understanding.

Dedicated: To All the Traders

ACKNOWLEDGEMENTS

When I started my journey as a trader, I had no idea it would lead me to write a handbook about my experience. I never set out to be an author, but as I continued to trade and learn more about the markets, I realised that I had accumulated a wealth of knowledge that could be helpful to other traders in taking the right decision.

From a nascent trader, who committed certain mistakes while making choices, to a seasoned trader, a lot of hard work was involved. My self-taught journey has allowed me to share my experience with others so that mistakes do not repeat and decisions are wiser.

I sincerely thank my parents, wife, and children for their constant support throughout the highs and lows of life. I would not be where I am today without their love and encouragement.

This book and none of what I do would be possible without my fantastic and talented IFMC® team members. I am thankful to my teachers and mentors who have guided me during my professional journey and made me the person I am.

Lastly, I thank the Almighty for bestowing me with a beautiful life and prayers to Him to keep me sane in all my endeavours.

ABOUT THE AUTHOR

Manish Taneja is a Senior Research Analyst at IFMC® Educational Institution Pvt. Ltd. He has more than 30 years of stock trading experience. He is known for his simple teaching methods on IFMC®'s YouTube Channel and at the Institute. His Copyrighted content Uni-Directional Trade Strategies©, with over 10 million views on YouTube, is popular in over 171 countries worldwide. He and his team are committed to creating stock trading courses and strategies that are very simple and easy to understand for a common person who wants to trade in the stock market. Their years of experience in the industry have given them the insight and knowledge to develop strategies that anyone can quickly follow without any prior experience or knowledge of the stock market. Their goal is to make trading accessible to everyone so that anyone can make a profit from the stock market simply by following the guided and disciplined approach.

People are generally afraid to invest in the stock market because of the inherent risk involved. Learning about the stock market is a distant dream for many people because it seems complex and intimidating. However, the lectures by Mr Manish Taneja are a great way to learn about the stock market. Mr. Taneja is a highly experienced and knowledgeable investor and a seasoned trader, and his lectures are a great way to gain insights into the stock market.

The unique selling preposition of his course, strategies, and lectures is simplicity. Thus, highly complicated topics and the subject become much easier to understand. His approach is designed to make it easy for the students to understand and apply the concepts in their daily lives.

From a simple small-town boy to a jobber to a professional trader to a respected mentor, his professional journey has been full of ups and downs, surviving significant hiccups in the market. He started his career as a jobber, buying and selling securities on behalf of clients, and then transitioned to trading for himself and later for his clients as a sub-broker making a living by buying and selling securities. Finally, after years of hard work and dedication, he became a professional trader, respected by his peers for his knowledge and insight into the markets. Today, he mentors other traders, helping them navigate the ups and downs of the markets.

He is now an inspiration to millions of traders who follow him worldwide for his copyright Strategies named - Uni-Directional Trade Strategies & Market Analysis by Data and Event (M.A.D.E.)

Accuracy and confidence are imparted to his students, who follow him diligently. The constant upgradation and learning from his mistakes and the ability to rise again after falling set him apart.

He is respected for his simplicity and down-to-earth approach to students and colleagues. From Ring Trading to Online Trading journey taken with passion has made him a prudent trader and mentor.

The Uni-Directional Trade Strategies© (UDTS©) is Mr. Manish Taneja's brainchild; his expertise has made simplified strategies in Intraday and Positional Trading. As a result, UDTS© is revolutionising trading by making it extremely simple for stock market beginners and traders around the globe. It has now globally grabbed the eyes of traders and industry players since its launch in April 2018.

FROM THE AUTHOR'S DESK

There is no substitute for experience, hard work, passion, and strong analytical skills in the stock market. There is no denying the fact that everyone wants to earn from it. Everyone wants profit, be it a small trader, an investor, or a High Net worth Individual (HNI). While there is no second opinion about it, the question is how to achieve this goal. However, the Stock Market is so volatile and slippery that traders and investors often end up misguided by their greed, thoughts, fear, and lack of experience and, most importantly, knowledge.

Learning and upgrading is the only way to survive in this market. I've been in the market for 30 years. I've seen it all, from the early days of ring trading to ever-advancing online trading platforms, where the speed of transactions has upped the ante.

People invest in the stock market for a variety of reasons. Some people invest to achieve financial security for their retirement, while others invest or trade to generate income.

The reasons to start trading are endless. It is a place of great opportunities where traders can make a fortune by correctly predicting which stocks will rise and fall in value.

However, the stock market has the potential to spell its curse, as it can just as easily destroy the accumulated wealth as it can create. The balance of yin and yang is the key. A sudden drop in the stock market can wipe out years of savings and investments, leaving people with nothing. Smart traders, on the other hand, are fearless of the market, as they take time to learn everything before they start trading.

Trading itself is a mammoth task. Intraday trading can be tricky; if you are not careful, you can easily end up losing money.

People have forgotten the 1992 Harshad Mehta fall, the 2000 IT Bubble Crash, the 2008 Subprime/Lehman Brother Crash, and the Global recession. I have witnessed all these three major jerks closely. Considering such events and experiences, my suggestion to make money from the stock market will be to trade from a safe distance. A safe distance because a minute mistake may result in generous losses. Do not be afraid; just respect the rallying of the index and earn with the right strategy, discipline, and specific rules. That is it!!! Do not run after the profits; they will come by themselves. Patience, my dear friend, patience.

I have attempted to explain everything I know in the most possible language in the book. I have also tried to explain the basics of stock trading differently, making it easy for beginners to master the UDTS© strategy that most people have never heard of.

I have included several case studies and examples to illustrate how these concepts can be applied in practice. I hope this book will give readers a helpful introduction to the world of the stock market and strategy with a completely different viewpoint and help them develop the skills and knowledge they need to succeed.

That is why

Think before you start trading!! Trade only when you have a perfect strategy in place. You also need to carefully analyse the market and have the conviction to hold the position when the market is against you.

UDTS© - The Brahmastra of Intraday Trading is a system that can help you achieve all of this. It is an excellent resource for developing a winning strategy. This book provides a step-by-step guide to creating a successful trading plan. It is packed with tips, advice, anecdotes, and words of wisdom to help you transform from a naive trader to a professional trader. Let us go ahead and read this book to change your trading perception and develop a better understanding of trading.

I aim to convert a normal trader to a UDTS© Smart Trader.

इंट्राडे ट्रेडिंग करनी है तो UDTS© आना ही चाहिए ।।

Happy Learning!!

Happy Trading!!

PREFACE

The more that you read, the more you know. The stock market is where information is never adequate, and many things are between the lines. The only thing which can be called black and white is the statistics accessible to all. Reading between the numbers and forming a decisive conclusion is an art.

My humble attempt is to make you understand the why, when, and what of the stock market, so you can make your own strategy for intraday calls. Reading and thorough understanding will help you set your own rules, which no technical analyst can rule out.

If you are ready to learn stock trading in a simple way, then this book is for you. I believe that by the end of the book, you will be able to trade confidently and have a clear understanding of the market without compromising on your emotions.

This handbook is essential for anyone who wants to master the art of trading without the need to learn cumbersome techniques. It lays out **UDTS©**, the Brahmastra of Intraday Trading, to trade like a professional trader. Whether you're a beginner or an experienced trader, this handbook will be a valuable resource.

The book will have some technical and some experiential parts. I have tried my best to simplify it all as much as possible at the request of my YouTube family. So, I hope this book makes you understand what the stock market is, what intraday trading is, why the market goes in the reverse direction whenever you buy or sell, and why the profits are always peanuts. Fundamentally, it's a guide on how to chase this mirage and come out as a winner. The only word of caution is that you should not be emotional and make all the decisions as per the strategy.

Every stock analyst has a unique way of seeing charts. While some use traditional methods like reading candlestick patterns, others might use more modern techniques like Fibonacci retracement levels. Just like every astrologer has their own individual way of making predictions, each stock analyst brings their own perspective to the table. One analyst might predict that a stock will go up, while another might predict that it will go down. It all depends on the analyst's unique method and interpretation.

In order to see the charts from the correct perspective, you need to re-engineer your brain. This may be difficult, but it is necessary to gain a new and accurate perspective. This new perspective will allow you to see the true nature of the charts and how they can be used to your advantage. Technical analysis is the key to success in the stock market, but you need to learn it with a clean slate.

The book is enriched with anecdotes and examples to simplify learning.

The book is an attempt to reach common people who want to learn Intraday Trading and want to trade profitably in the stock market without taking any paid tips or calls from the market. It is a comprehensive guide for beginners & traders. No prior knowledge of technical fundamentals is required. It is a simple way to trade for a common man.

For better understanding, the reader can go through the complete online programme of Uni-Directional Trade Strategies© by IFMC® Educational Institution Pvt Ltd. We highly suggest practising paper trade and understanding our strategies competently before applying them to the live market. It allows you to imbibe how our strategy works and how applicable it is in real-world situations.

THE STOCK MARKET IS EASY WHEN YOU KNOW-HOW

I genuinely believe stock trading is easy when you know how. Step by step journey will guide you toward your objective. Before venturing into trading, clear your basics, devise a successful strategy, and lastly, gain key-point practice and experience.

Going further, we will find detailed chapters on Uni-Directional Trade Strategies©. For a better understanding of the strategy, the chapters are divided into three parts— Basics, Analytics and Applicability.

BASICS

In Basics, we will try to understand what a trader has to keep in mind before understanding the strategy to get the best outcome. In this section, we will learn in detail about the need for a trading Brahamstra, the four tactical weapons, and ten golden rules, i.e., market behaviour, market perils, eligibility to understand the UDTS© strategy, the difference between an investor and a trader, the difference between a gambler and a trader, trading is an art, why do we need a trading strategy, and why technical analysis is cumbersome for a common man, intraday trading and the difference between intraday & positional trading and different time frame charts.

ANALYTICS

In Analytics, you will learn about candles. Candlestick charts can provide a wealth of information about market sentiment, price action, and much more. The candles provide inputs that can be used to make decisions about buying or selling a stock. When you look at the candles, you can forecast the direction of the market, the strength of the trend, and the level of activity. We will also learn how to see candles differently, as charts have a particular language, and to know what a candle is saying, you must know the language of the candle charts. Every stock analyst has a unique way of seeing charts. While some use traditional methods like reading candlestick patterns, others might use more modern techniques like Fibonacci retracement levels. Just like every astrologer has their own individual way of making predictions, each stock analyst brings their own perspective to the table. One analyst might predict that a stock will go up, while another might predict that it will go down. It all depends on the analyst's unique method and interpretation.

In order to see the charts from the correct perspective, you need to re-engineer your brain. This may be difficult, but it is necessary in order to gain a new and accurate perspective. This new perspective will allow you to see the true nature of the charts and how they can be used to your advantage. Technical analysis is the key to success in the stock market, but you need to learn it with a clean slate.

You will also learn how to make a view from fundamental and technical analysis.

APPLICABILITY

Friends, even after learning many big tools of technical analysis, many people fail because emotions overpower them in the live market and difficulty in applying cumbersome technical tools. As a result, the overall learning gets diluted when it comes to applicability in the live market. My advice is to be more practical and then theoretical.

In the applicability section, you will learn how to do intraday & short positional trading applying the UDTS© strategy. We have also designed a Trade Model for our readers for better applicability. By applying the proper strategy, you can win your emotions while trading. Finally, you will learn an ideal intraday trading model so that you can achieve the highest probability of winning and become a successful intraday trader.

Get... Set... Go...

WHAT TO EXPECT?
THE OUTCOME OF LEARNING

When you read this handbook on trading, you can expect to learn various trading aspects in-depth. These skills will help you understand the stock market like a professional trader.

You can then use this knowledge to decide when to buy or sell stocks and how to manage your portfolio best. By the end of this book, you'll be able to learn how to:

- View the market with more clarity
- Monetise data and news analysis
- Learn to find the proper entry and exit levels of stocks
- Learn to calculate support and resistance
- Improve the probability of winning trades
- Set stop-losses and targets with accuracy
- Manage emotions like a professional trader
- Trade with 100% confidence

Let's Begin

TABLES OF CONTENT

Disclaimer of Warranties and Limitation of Liability vii
Acknowledgements ix
About the Author xi
From the Author's Desk xiii
Preface xv
The Stock Market is easy when you know-How xvii
    Basics xvii
    Analytics xvii
    Applicability xviii
What to expect? The outcome of learning xix
Tables of Content xxi

PART A
Basics of Uni-Directional Trade Strategies©

Chapter 1
UDTS© Brahmastra - Empowering Trader Skills 3

Chapter 2
Enter the Stock Market with Proper Skills 5

Chapter 3

4 Tactical Weapons and 10 Golden Rules Of UDTS©....................7

    3.1 Four Weapons of a Trader 7

        Weapon 1. Knowledge of demand and supply 8

        Weapon 2. The trend is your ultimate friend 8

        Weapon 3. Confidence in yourself and your strategy 8

        Weapon 4. Practice and experience 9

    3.2 Ten Golden Rules of UDTS© strategy 9

        Rule 1: Always stick to your category: drive in your lane. 9

        Rule 2: Emotions can harm your judgment. 10

        Rule 3: Hedge Your Position Always. 11

        Rule 4: Patience is a virtue for profitable trade 12

        Rule 5: Always sell in falling markets and buy in rising markets Or Never buy in falling markets and never sell in rising markets 13

        Rule 6: Never do Averaging... 13

        Rule 7: Quality Trades 14

        Rule 8: Stop-loss is a must - Risk Management 15

        Rule 9: Trading Only in A & B Group 15

        Rule 10: Never trade in a single stock 16

Chapter 4

Traders Beware of Market Perils 17

    Peril 1 17

    Peril 2 20

Chapter 5

Qualities & Eligibility to Become UDTS© Trader........................ 22

    Qualities of a successful trader 22

    How I discovered my analytical skills—an interesting story 22

    Common mistakes of a trader (Investor vs Trader) 23

Chapter 6

Trading is a Game of Probability 25

Chapter 7
Why Do We Need A Trading Strategy? 28
    Trading Strategy for Different Goals 29

Chapter 8
Need for a simple strategy without cumbersome tools of Technical Analysis 31

Chapter 9
Uni-Directional Trade Strategies© 33
    Accuracy of UDTS© Strategy 36

Chapter 10
UDTS© - A Skill for Monetising Market Behaviour 37

Chapter 11
Different Trading Styles 39
    Intraday Trading 40
    Positional Trading 42
    Swing Trading 43
    Long Position Trading 43
    What are the critical differences between intraday and positional trading? 44
    Difference between Intraday, Short-Term Positional (Swing), Medium-Term Positional (Swing), and Long-Term Positional Trading 45

Chapter 12
Different Time Frame Charts for Trading 47
    Right Time-Frame charts for intraday trading? 48
    Confident traders are either bulls or bears on a particular day. 49

PART B
Analytics of Uni-Directional Trade Strategies©

Chapter 13
How to make the view from fundamentals? 53
    Bullish or Bearish View 53
    Data Analysis 55

Chapter 14
Making Trading View with Trend Analysis 63
    What is a Candle & how do you Read Candles? 63
    What is a trend, and how to view trends on candles? 67
        Monthly Trend 68
        Weekly Trend 69
        Daily Trend 70

PART C
Applicability of UDTS©

Chapter 15
Intraday Trading Strategies On Candles 77
    Bullish Parameters 77
        First Parameter (EOD or End of the Day Parameter) 77
        Second Parameter (EOD or End-Of-The-Day Parameter) 78
        Third Parameter (EOD or End-Of-The-Day Parameter) 79
        Fourth Parameter (EOD or End-Of-The-Day Parameter) 80
        Fifth Parameter (Intraday Parameter) 81
        Sixth Parameter 82
    Stop-loss as per UDTS© strategy 92
    What should be the targets as per UDTS© principles? 93

No Trade Before 10 a.m. 94
Unchallenged points of entry and exit 94
The biggest trend of the day 95
Definition of support and resistance as per UDTS© Principles 96
What is the meaning of sustenance? 98
    Sustenance time for monthly support or resistance 98
    Sustenance time for weekly support or resistance 99
    Sustenance time for daily support or resistance 99
GAP-UP or GAP-DOWN Opening 100
Trading Concepts 100
    1. Trade Like a Thief 101
    2. Always Stay Behind Bull or Bear Whoever is
       more powerful 102

Chapter 16
Short-Term Positional Trading Strategy On Candles 104

Chapter 17
Medium-Term Positional Trading Strategy on Candles 108

Chapter 18
Long-Term Positional trading strategy on candles 109

Chapter 19
Trade Model-To Achieve Regular Income from Intraday
Trading 110
    Step 1 – Making view by News and Data 112
    Step 2 - Technical view on NIFTY 112
    Step 3 - Making a basket 113
    Step 4 - Sectoral Analysis 114
    Step 5 - Stock selection as per the six parameters of UDTS© 114

Chapter 20

Why UDTS© Better Than AI-Based Trading Software? 115

    AI software is fully dependent on technical analysis tools 115

    Stop-losses on software utilities are predictable 115

    AI software utilities are to make brokerages for brokers 116

    Software utilities don't have experience as humans 117

Chapter 21

Common questions in the mind of traders/FAQs 118

    1. When I sell, the market goes up. 118

    2. When I buy, the market goes down. 119

    3. I am fed up with the stock market; my luck is terrible in the stock market 119

    4. Whenever I trade, my profits are peanuts, but my losses are enormous 119

    5. Lastly, a common Complaint: The index is rising and touching new highs, but my portfolio is always down. 120

Author's Story 121

    1. Stock market has been my destiny 121

    2. My journey in primary, as well as a secondary market to ring trading 122

    3. Working in the ring was a different experience 123

    4. Realisation of analytical skills 123

    5. Market taught me the actual meaning of discipline. 124

    6. I lost my job, and trading was my only livelihood. 124

    7. Manual trading to online trading— the golden period 124

    8. When traders started believing my ideology 125

    9. The dot-com bubble incident was a blow to my confidence and learning 125

    10. Gathered courage and sharpened learnings to be a prudent trader 127

    11. My emotional outburst 128

    12. As a mentor. 129

13. Started formal education for traders.. 129
14. The making of UDTS©... 129
15. On viewer's demand... 130

UDTS© Became the Best Online Selling Course in India............. 131

Why do I like this profession? 132

Folklore Of Greed And Fear In The Trading Community
The Greedy Ghanshyam... 133

PART A

BASICS OF UNI-DIRECTIONAL TRADE STRATEGIES©

CHAPTER 1
UDTS© BRAHMASTRA - EMPOWERING TRADER SKILLS

Diminishing demons of fear, anxiety, uncertainty, emotions, and greed

Everyone who has ever traded or is trading in the stock market has gone through the feeling of being lost in the market. Everyone, at some point in time, makes losses and feels anxiety, depression, and fear. It's easy to lose all your money when you have come up with the expectation of making money from the market.

There is always a need for unbeatable "MANTRA" for a trader so that he doesn't lose hard-earned money in the Stock Market. A trader must have some miracle power that carves wonders for him and defines his winning streaks.

Thus, let us dedicate some time to understanding the complexities of the stock market simply and earn a "POWER" that is unbeatable.

Brahmastra is a Sanskrit word that means the "Weapon of Brahma." In Hindu mythology, it is considered the most powerful weapon in the universe.

The Brahmastra is said to be a weapon that Lord Brahma created. The Gods used it in their battles against the demons. The weapon is also said to be able to be used by humans, but only for good deeds. As no tool can overpower Brahmastra, similarly, no Technical Tool can overpower UDTS© - The Ultimate tool for all stock market woes.

This tool diminishes the demons of fear, anxiety, uncertainties, emotions, and greed and helps the trader to remain in control.

To possess this Brahmastra, you are required to grasp the concepts thoroughly and with no preconceived notions of older ways of stock trading, then only will you be able to transform yourself from a common trader to a skilled UDTS© trader. Your transformational journey begins now.

UDTS© brings an end to all stock market woes.

CHAPTER 2
ENTER THE STOCK MARKET WITH PROPER SKILLS

95% of people never earn from the stock market due to a lack of skill and practice. It is why it's integral to educate yourself about both—rewards and risks—before considering trading. For quick money, beginners resort to intraday trading, a tricky business where the minutest of carelessness can lead to significant losses. That's why it is important to have a solid strategy in place.

The stock market has been a place of intrigue and fascination for 200 years. It is like a **'Mayajaal'.** People come to the stock market to maximise returns but underestimate the volatile state as its basic essence. It can make someone richer or poorer overnight.

The pandemic of 2020 transformed the stock market scenario radically. Primarily because more and more people found this as an avenue for earnings, to supplement income, which either was reduced or nullified during difficult times. The market experienced an upsurge by attracting common people and retailers. Call it beginner's luck for some, but NIFTY was hovering around 8,000–11,000 then, which, in October 2022 (when I was writing the book), scaled to 18,000. As a result, people made massive profits, which helped mellow down the losses (to some extent) suffered during the lockdown period. Many traders earned a return of more than 100% in many stocks in 1-2 years, creating a gravitational pull for new entrants considering trading as a full-time profession.

Coming off the COVID bottom, the market rallied feverishly, and it was easy for many traders to reap the rewards. During this time, just about every stock, good or bad, seemed to rally due to FOMO (Fear of Missing Out). It's great that many people have taken their financial security seriously. Many investors and traders follow guidance from individuals on social platforms, through news articles, and, of course, from friends and family.

The market started declining in 2022, and profits started evaporating. Experienced traders and investors could lock in the bulk of their earnings because they knew what and when to do or, for that matter, act timely with changing market dynamics. However, many budding traders learn the tough lessons of the trade. Hearing from these, I could gauge where they could have gone wrong. They didn't have a proper plan or the skills to determine when to buy, what to buy, and, most importantly, when to sell.

The **UDTS© - The Brahmastra of Intraday Trading** is a great resource for developing a winning strategy. It provides a step-by-step guide for creating a successful trading plan and a wealth of tips and advice from the author's desk.

CHAPTER 3

4 TACTICAL WEAPONS AND 10 GOLDEN RULES OF UDTS©

The stock market is a fierce battle between buyers and sellers, impatient and patient, knowledgeable and spontaneous.

Before we start the journey of learning, I am arming traders with these four weapons and ten rules to help them succeed in the market. These weapons and rules are the key to success and will help traders make money. With these in hand, traders can make a killing in the market. These weapons are a strong work ethic, dedication to learning, a positive attitude, and a willingness to take risks. By following these rules and arming yourself with these weapons, you will be well on your way to becoming a successful trader.

3.1 FOUR WEAPONS OF A TRADER

The four must-have weapons of a trader that will help them become a more successful and profitable trader are:

1. Knowledge of demand and supply
2. Stay with the trend as "Trend is your ultimate friend"
3. Confidence in yourself and your strategy
4. Practice and experience

These weapons have served me well over the years. I believe they can benefit any trader willing to do the work. All traders must be well-versed in these four weapons and skill sets. By understanding and utilising all four of these weapons, traders can give themselves a significant advantage in the market. With the proper knowledge and tools, a trader can be well on their way to ultimate success.

Weapon 1. Knowledge of demand and supply

In the world of trading, knowledge is power. The key to successful trading is knowledge of demand and supply, as these are the primary factors affecting price movements in the market. Demand and supply are the two most important factors driving market price movements. By understanding how these two factors interact, traders can better understand where prices will likely go upward in the future. When demand is high and supply is low, the price will go up. The price will go down when demand is low, and supply is high.

Traders who understand demand and supply can use this knowledge to their advantage. By anticipating how these two factors will interact, traders can make informed decisions about when to enter and exit the markets.

The right forecast of demand and supply for the next 3-4 hours in intraday trading can make a trader an ace trader.

Weapon 2. The trend is your ultimate friend

Another critical point to remember for successful trading is that "Trend is your ultimate friend". Staying with the trend and following it can lead to success in trading, allowing you to ride the wave of momentum and profit from it. The trend is the best indicator of where the market is headed. If the demand is high, position yourself on the side of demand to take advantage of the situation. Similarly, if the supply is high, align yourself on the side of the supply so that you can benefit from the excess. By being aware of the current market trend, you can position yourself in a way that maximises your chances of success.

Weapon 3. Confidence in yourself and your strategy

Trading is successful only when you have faith in your strategy. You might lose the game completely if you lack confidence in your script. Before making a trade, be confident in yourself and your strategy. Taking an exit from the trade is in your best interest if you are not confident enough.

Along with confidence, traders must know how to deliver a master stroke. This means that for a batsman to hit a six, he needs to hit the ball with complete confidence; slightly less than complete confidence may get him caught before the boundary wall.

Only when a trader is one hundred percent confident should one enter the trade; believe me, seventy to eighty percent of the work is already done. To be a successful stock trader, you must be confident in your ability, so start building your confidence today by taking the first step toward getting educated and trained in this area.

Weapon 4. Practice and experience

Practice, practice, and practice!!! Practice makes a trader perfect!

Preparation leads to power. The old warrior's mantra, "The more sweat you shed in training, the less you bleed in battle", also applies here, i.e., the greater the preparation, the greater the ability to handle adversity, and the stronger the partnership develops.

These four weapons will surely help the traders while applying the strategy to get perfect results.

3.2 TEN GOLDEN RULES OF UDTS© STRATEGY

There are rules in every game for a reason, as without rules, there can be no game. And the stock market is no different—if you break the rules, you will lose. Thus, it's essential to know the rules and follow them accordingly. These rules will raise your winning probability, so it's important to always stick to them and be loyal to them. Ten golden trading rules which a trader or an investor must imbibe into your mind to be a successful trader.

Rule 1: Always stick to your category: drive in your lane.

The first rule is to trade in only one category. This simply means that whether you are an intraday, positional, or long-positional trader, make sure you do not change categories and only focus on one type of trading. This will help you stay disciplined and raise your chances of success.

In intraday, the stop-loss is less, and so is the target; in positional trade, the stop-loss is more significant, and the target is also bigger. Mixing categories will reduce your earnings and forfeit your objective.

If you are an intraday trader, you must remember that you will only be holding your position for a while. And if you are a positional trader, you will not enter or exit a trade during the intraday.

For example: If you purchase a share for ₹100 and the stop-loss is ₹98 in the evening, and if the price falls to ₹95, which is lower than the stop-loss, and if you do not cut your position in the evening and carry your position overnight, you have ensured further losses for next day. Here you entered the trade as an intraday trader but converted your position to positional trade as you do not have enough courage to book the loss at your stop-loss price of ₹98, and you stand beside the hopes that may be the stock rise again to cover your losses next day. Here you are purely gambling and relying on luck.

An intraday trader must remain an intraday trader, and a long positional trader must remain a long positional trader, as views for targets and stop-loss are different for different goals. There are many kinds of traders in the market, but each must stick to their own trading style to succeed. Traders often try to switch styles to take advantage of different market conditions, which usually leads to disaster. It is much better to remain focused on one's own trading strategy and stick to it no matter what.

In a nutshell, do not ever mix your category in the flow of emotions. If your stop-loss is hitting intraday trade, square up your trade and book the loss. Do not carry the trade for the next day, assuming the stock will rise tomorrow.

If you are a long positional trader, do not cut your trade by making small profits if you get it the same day.

Rule 2: Emotions can harm your judgment.

Another rule of trading is to keep your emotions in check. It's not always easy to remain calm in the face of adversity. But if you can learn to keep your emotions in check, you'll be a better trader and more likely to succeed in the long run.

You need to be able to separate your emotions from your stocks. I have emphasised many times that a trader is someone who sees an opportunity and seizes it. You can't get too attached to any particular stock, even if it's performing well. You need to be able to sell quickly if the opportunity arises. Getting too attached will only blind you from other opportunities and prevent you from making a profit.

Traders get attached to a position and watch it fall instead of selling it.

Example: A trader buys a stock at ₹100, but now it has fallen to ₹90. He still keeps it; rather, he buys more to make an average because he heard positive news about the stock from his friends. Now it falls again to ₹80, and gradually it comes to ₹9 or ₹10, but he still keeps the bond. But his capital will be finished. In the stock market, emotions can be very dangerous for traders. They can lead to impulsive decisions that can harm your investment portfolio. It is important to trade emotionlessly without letting emotions get into your decision-making. This can be difficult, but it is essential to succeed in the stock market. When you allow your emotions to takeover, you are more likely to make decisions based on fear or greed rather than logic and reason. This can lead to costly mistakes. So, remember to stay calm and focused when trading, and do not let your emotions get the best of you.

Rule 3: Hedge Your Position Always.

This will help to mitigate risk and protect your investments. This is a fundamental rule in trading because it allows you to minimise risk. You are essentially buying insurance against a potential loss by hedging your position. No matter which way you choose to hedge your position, always remember to do so before a big event. By doing so, you can protect yourself from a potentially catastrophic loss.

There are a few different ways to hedge your position. One way to hedge is to use derivatives such as options contracts or futures contracts. Another way is to use physical assets such as gold or silver.

Example: Suppose you are carrying a long overnight position. In that case, you should consider hedging it because, during the day, there is less need to hedge it since you are sitting in front of the trading window and can quit anytime. Always remember to use a stop-loss!!

However, we sleep with our eyes open when we take any overnight position to the next day. We trust the market will not move against us too much overnight and that we will not get stopped. This is risky but can pay off if we are careful and disciplined in our trading. Markets are very dynamic. If we sleep, even then, the markets are moving globally, and we never know what will happen at night that we have to face in the morning when the market opens.

Rule 4: Patience is a virtue for profitable trade

Patience is key to any successful trading strategy. Those who are patient in their investments are often rewarded with healthy returns, as they can ride out the market's fluctuations and capitalise on opportunities. On the other hand, those who lack patience often sell their investments at a loss, as they panic when the market takes a dip.

Patience as a quality is to be practised while you are on the profitable side; as soon as you are in red or hit stop-loss, it's better to exit with minimal losses. Suppose you bought a stock for ₹100, and the stock keeps falling to 90… 80… 50 before stabilising, and you did not quit waiting for the stock price to rise above ₹100. Then you are no more a trader. You have become an investor. As a trader, you already incurred an escalated loss of ₹50 from ₹100 if your stop-loss was ₹90.

But friends, I do not call this investment an investment for traders. I believe you are stuck with this stock because, whatever you have purchased, you could not avail yourself of the opportunity to exit it before minimising your loss. You can't do anything except patiently wait for the price to rebound.

So finally, friends, remember that the patience we are talking about is only when your trades are profitable and not when you are trapped. Minimise your loss, and do not block your investment.

Rule 5: Always sell in falling markets and buy in rising markets Or Never buy in falling markets and never sell in rising markets

This rule might appear awkward to you, but yes, it is most important when it comes to intraday trading.

The key to making money in the market lies in mastering the fine art of buying low and selling high. Yep. That's it in a nutshell! However, as anyone who has ever traded in the market knows, it's much easier said than done.

Actually, the truth is that no one can catch the lowest or highest points of the market.

If a stock is going down in momentum and you ride the stock at any price, you will find yourself below your buying price of yours after some time. Similarly, if you sell a rising stock, you will find a higher price after some time of selling the stock.

So, when is the right time to buy stock at a low price? Plain and simple—wait until it has stopped going down and started going up. And you do not do it immediately, but make sure the stock is well on its way up, and then you jump on and enjoy the ride.

In a nutshell, buy only when the stock has upward momentum and sell only when it has started to have downward momentum.

Rule 6: Never do Averaging

Averaging is a stock trading strategy that involves buying a security at regular intervals to reduce the overall cost basis of the security. The idea is that over time, the security will go up in value, and the cost basis will be lower, resulting in a profit when the security is sold. However, there are several problems inherent to averaging. Many traders have lost their entire capital using this strategy without adequate knowledge.

Suppose a trader bought a stock for ₹100, and then when the stock fell to ₹85, he bought more. And when it fell to ₹80 or ₹75, he added more at a lower price. Ultimately, when the price fell to ₹50 or ₹20, he lost 80% of all his capital. So never average your stocks if you do not know how to manage them.

Average trading should be done only till the stock price is above your stop-loss levels. For example, I buy a stock for ₹100, and my stop-loss is ₹90. When it falls to ₹97, I may buy some more. If it falls to ₹92, I can buy more stocks because it is still above my stop-loss.

But if it falls to ₹89, I have to quit all my positions, and there is no need to average below ₹90. Averaging is a stock trading strategy you should use only when you are fully aware of it.

Rule 7: Quality Trades

When it comes to trading, always remember to value quality trades over quantity trades. Trade only when your trade has the highest probability of winning; otherwise, do not do it. At times, people trade by guesswork, leading to either immense profits or huge losses. Contrary to professional trading, this simply is gambling. Professional traders always have an objective of bringing some money home as it's their bread and butter. The focus should be on specific trades with a high chance of success.

Moreover, if you are trading more, you are giving more brokerages and taxes to brokers and reducing your earnings. So work for yourself, not for your broker. Based on the trading pattern, it can be judged whether someone is gambling or trading.

Let us take an example:

Person A did 5 intraday trades, making +2% -1% +1% -1.5% +1.5% = 2%,

Whereas Person B did 11 intraday trades, making +4% +6% -8% -8% -7% +5% +5% -8% +7% -6% -5% = -15%

Here A is taking profits and losses not above 2% to 3% in any intraday trade by doing only 5 trades and at least adding 2% to his net. At the same time, B took 11 trades and took 8% to 9% profits and losses in all his trades, with a resulting loss of 15% in a single day. Here, A is trading with minimum risk quality trades as a professional trader aiming to make a profit. Whereas B is gambling, taking too much risk on single trades and concentrating on quantity rather than quality trades.

Rule 8: Stop-loss is a must - Risk Management

Stop-loss determines your risk-to-reward ratio. If your stop-loss is too large compared to your targets, your risk-to-reward ratio will be too high, and you will likely lose money on the trade. Conversely, if your stop-loss is as per your targets, your risk-to-reward ratio will be high, and you will likely make money on the trade. Therefore, it is important to always know the stop-loss before entering a trade so that you can manage your risks accordingly. Never enter a trade where your stop-loss is higher than your targets. To be precise, I recommend not taking a trade with a stop-loss of over 2% in intraday trading.

For example, if the stock price is ₹100 and the stop-loss is at ₹95, here your risk is almost 5%; you must wait to take the position if the stock further falls to 96 to 97, then only start looking for other parameters to meet so you can enter the trade. Once the strategy gives a green signal near this price, you can enter the trade with full confidence. Now you are taking the trade at 97 with almost 2% of stop-loss.

So rather than taking the risk of 5%, you have taken the risk of only 2%. So, in a nutshell, risk management by stop-loss is an integral part of the strategy, but yes, you should know what the right stop-loss for your trade will be. That will be covered in detail in later chapters.

Rule 9: Trading Only in A & B Group

Group A companies have a market cap greater than ₹20,000 crores, while Group B companies have a market cap between ₹5000 and ₹20,000 crores. It is advised to trade in these companies as there is good liquidity, and operators are not able to take advantage of retailers. One also sees lesser chances of upper circuits and lower circuits in these stocks. Thus, safety in these stocks is higher. In contrast, penny stocks have a lower market capitalisation and are more risk prone. Operators also take undue advantage of traders trading in penny stocks.

Do not trade in penny stocks, as they can lead to heavy losses in intraday because these stocks are heavily volatile with lesser volumes, and they do not have much equity. On these penny stocks, Bulls and

Beer Cartel (a group of people who manipulate stock prices) can easily have their grip because such stocks have smaller equity and can be easily manipulated, and as a result, retail traders find themselves stuck in such stocks by paying heavy losses. The most dangerous part of trading penny stocks is that they can freeze at any time in the upper or lower circuit. The exchange has a set limit for each stock for its intraday rise and fall; once this limit is crossed, the stock will freeze, and no trading can happen further. So if a trader has bought a stock at ₹10, and it freezes at the lower circuit at ₹9, you can't sell that stock intraday, and you have to take compulsory delivery of that stock. Yes, you can sell the stock the next day. But in such stocks, operators play foul, and many times you may notice that its frozen state does not open for the next 6 to 8 days. By this time, the stock price will drop from ₹2 to ₹3. Now you have lost 70% of your money in this intraday trade to earn just 2% to 3%.

So never fall prey to such stocks. Avoid them as a good trader. It's always better to trade in A and B group stocks that are less volatile and have more liquidity.

Rule 10: Never trade in a single stock

If you are doing intraday trading. Even after applying a good strategy and all the rules, you must think of better probabilities. Even if you have the potential to win in 8 out of 10 trades, there are still 2 trades that can give you losses. And when you do a single trade and lose, you end up with losses. Professional traders never rely on a single trade; instead, they try to make a basket of trades so that if one trade doesn't work, another will help in covering the losses. Like a cliché of not putting all eggs in one basket, do not put all your trading amount in a single trade.

Before trading, learn strategies and follow them. This is because no game can be played without rules. By understanding and adopting these 10 trading rules, you will be able to trade more effectively and improve your chances of success.

CHAPTER 4
TRADERS BEWARE OF MARKET PERILS

After learning the weapons and rules of UDTS©, as a mentor, it's my duty to tell you about the perils of stock trading also. You do not have to be afraid of these perils when you know how to manage and mitigate risks. Being aware is the key so that whenever you trade, you are in full control of all the consequences. An informed and learned trader always takes full precautions to save both his invested capital and profits.

The two main perils are:

PERIL 1

80% of the trading portfolio can be washed in a single day, but when will doomsday come? No one knows. Always Maintain a Safe distance from the market.

The market is brutal to those who do not obey its dynamism or act imprudently and greedily. The Stock Market is a one-stop destination for the multiplication of money. Traders blindly start trading in markets after seeking help from friends or relationship managers. Traders often become overconfident and do not sharpen their weapons and practical skills. It is the biggest mistake they commit, and they lose everything.

There is an inherent lust for money in every human being. Of all living creatures on Earth, the human being is the only living creature that needs money for survival. In contrast, all other creatures need a life. This is the bitter irony of human existence.

People have always been on a quest to explore possibilities of a second income, be it from savings or investment in any available financial instrument, ever since the trade practices brought a new dimension of exchanges in currency or valuables so that money keeps growing even when they are sleeping. Everyone dreams of an ever-blooming **MONEY TREE** or **KUBER KA KHAZANA.** People do everything they can to multiply the money and come to the stock market without experience.

Most of them get a bitter experience, as, instead of RAGS TO RICHES, the story is snake reversed to RICHES TO RAGS. Instead of being rich overnight, they lose everything in a day.

This reminds me of a snake and ladder game. Even the good player is bitten by a snake at 98 and returns to 8 from where he started his journey.

Thus, take every move with caution after clearly understanding all the signals.

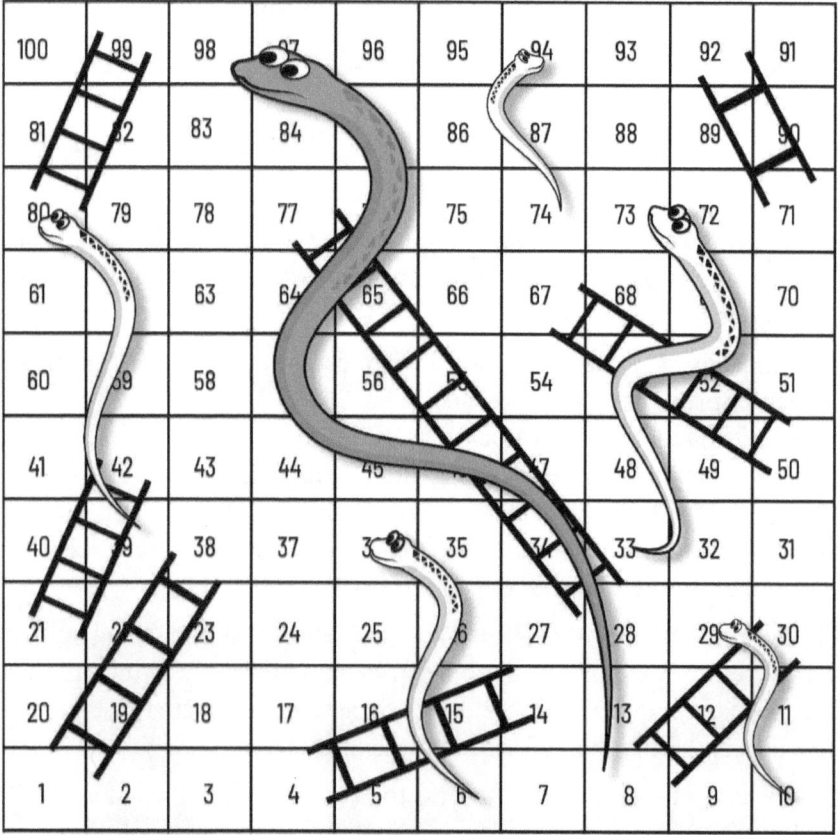

In my childhood, I had heard an imaginary story of an animal that slept for an extended period. People thought it was a stable ground to build a village and started living merrily. But when the animal woke up, it engulfed the entire town, leaving nothing.

The stock market is also like a huge animal that often lays dormant for an extended period, coiling in its sleep. Many people mistake it for stable ground and build their homes on it. But when this creature rises from slumber, it destroys whoever is in its vicinity.

The market is suitable for all those who respect it and keep a **safe distance** from it, but it's destructive for those who are greedy and stubborn and keep no distance from it.

SAFE DISTANCE means traders should never trade with their entire capital at a particular point, and investors should balance their portfolio between stocks and debt instruments, keeping a safer distance from the stock market, because no one knows when this creature will wake up next and create havoc in the market, as we have already seen in 1992, 2000, and 2008. With god's grace, this creature has been coiled in its sleep since 2008.

PERIL 2

"Traders are cursed." This saying is based on my personal experience that a trader forgets all his learnings whenever they experience losses.

We have often seen or read in mythology that the characters often bear the brunt of a curse, sometimes during their lifetime and sometimes even after death. Similarly, all traders and investors in the stock market are living with a curse. I am also no exception to the curse.

However, I make sure that I carry protection against the curse whenever I enter the market. Let us understand what the curse is:

Whenever the trader makes losses, he will forget all his learnings. People may laugh it off, but as a trader in the stock market for the last 30 years, I have experienced this curse. All those who have worked in the stock market at any point understand this curse. Once a trader starts getting losses, he forgets the strategy he has to follow; rather, he starts trading with his emotions and destroys his hard-earned wealth. Prudent traders know that loss is an integral part of trading, and if you are coming to trade in the market for profits, you have to accept the losses too. Traders should have enough guts to cut their losses at the very first opportunity. Not to wait if the market goes in the reverse direction. By cutting your losses at the right time, you can save your big losses. In a nutshell, even in losses, you should not leave the strategy and follow it with full discipline to eliminate this curse.

This belief is based on the fact that losses can be emotionally devastating and can cause a trader to question everything they know. When a trader is in the midst of a losing streak, it can be very difficult to stay calm and focused. It is during these times that a trader is most likely to make rash and impulsive decisions that can lead to even more losses.

The saying "traders are cursed" is a reminder to always stay disciplined and focused, even when things are going bad. It is important to remember that losses are a part of trading and that they can happen to even the most experienced and successful traders. What separates successful traders from losers is their ability to learn from their mistakes and to keep a cool head when things are going against them.

Traders have the curse of forgetting to use their knowledge whenever they need it the most, just like the 'KARAN' of Mahabharat. Karan was a great warrior of his time, but he eventually forgot how to use his weapon and was killed by Arjun.

By now, you must have understood the stock market's perils. In the coming chapters, we will discuss how to be a successful UDTS© trader.

CHAPTER 5

QUALITIES & ELIGIBILITY TO BECOME UDTS© TRADER

Traders are individuals or professionals involved in buying and selling stocks and securities. All traders attempt to profit from the sale and purchase of securities such as stocks or shares.

People invest a lot of time and effort to understand the stock market and financial instruments; however, they fail to understand the virtues of a trader. A clear understanding of a trader will help you work in the market with more ease and help you become a successful and professional trader.

QUALITIES OF A SUCCESSFUL TRADER

To become a successful trader, one must have several qualities. Some of the most crucial attributes of traders are:

1. **Common Sense:** Firstly, you need to have common sense. You need to be able to think logically and make sound decisions, even under pressure.
2. **Analytics Mind:** Secondly, you need strong analytical skills. This means understanding and interpreting data and making predictions based on your analysis.

Both of these qualities are necessary for a successful trader. In my opinion, there is no other degree course to become a successful trader.

HOW I DISCOVERED MY ANALYTICAL SKILLS—AN INTERESTING STORY

In 1992, I entered the stock market in my second graduation year. Before that, I tried my hands at various competitive exams, and, as expected, I failed. I had no option but to join graduation, that too under family pressure to at least be a graduate. However, I had no interest in doing anything, and the job was also a way to remain engaged and bring some money back home. I was an average student and lost faith in my studies and in doing anything constructive. The stock market came to me as a chance as our neighbours were stock brokers in the Delhi Stock exchange. Since I was an undergraduate student, due to the persuasion of my parents, they kept me as an intern.

Due to my full-time job, it was difficult to concentrate on my studies, and going to college for studies never interested me. However, I was very nervous when exams arrived, so I took a shortcut—I bought the previous year's question papers to prepare from the FAQs and checked their patterns.

I started analysing the questions asked in previous years' exams, looked for patterns to predict which questions would likely be asked in future examinations, and found that specific topics were often tested, so I focused my studies on those areas.

After completing my analysis, I could narrow my focus to four or five questions and chapters. So I studied them intensely. When I appeared for the exam, I was surprised that I cleared it on the first attempt. That was a turning point in my life. It automatically led to my success in the second year, and finally, I graduated.

Soon I realised I have a natural aptitude for analytics, and if I hone this skill, I can make loads of money from the stock market. Though I wasn't the best student academically, I have learned a lot in the market from my mistakes and successes. I have made a great deal of money and lost a lot, but overall, I have come out ahead.

COMMON MISTAKES OF A TRADER (INVESTOR VS TRADER)

A trader often forgets "Who he is". He loses his identity as soon as he enters the stock market. Sometimes he acts and behaves like an investor, and sometimes, as a trader, he keeps changing lanes. Finally, he gets stuck and becomes a zero from a hero.

People often ask me what the difference is between investors and traders. While both groups are involved in the stock market, there are some key differences between the two. The main difference between investors and traders is their time horizon. Investors are in it for the long haul and focused more on the fundamentals of the stocks, looking to buy and hold onto assets for years or even decades. Traders, on the other hand, are much more focused on the demand and supply of the stocks through technical charts; they are opportunistic and short-term oriented, frequently buying and selling assets within days or hours.

Another key difference is risk tolerance. Investors are generally more risk-averse than traders, as they are typically more focused on preserving capital and growing it slowly over time. On the other hand, traders are often more willing to take risks in pursuit of quick profits.

Lastly, investors are on the passive side, while traders are on the active side. Investors often buy assets and then hold onto them, while traders constantly monitor the markets, looking for opportunities to buy or sell.

- **Never mix trading with investing**
- **Investing is long-term | Trading is short-term**

An investor has a long-term perspective, whereas a trader has a short-term perspective. The investor will look more into the basics of the company and its fundamental parameters, whereas the trader will look more into its technical parameters.

Trader	Investor
• Short-term • Study technical charts • Opportunistic • Active returns	• Long-term • Fundamentals • Loyal share holder • Passive returns

CHAPTER 6
TRADING IS A GAME OF PROBABILITY

Are stock traders gamblers?

Traders are not gamblers; they are opportunistic. But yes, if you enter the market without knowledge, then, of course, it's gambling.

Let me explain it to you with an example:

We all know the story of Mahabharata, where Pandavas lost everything to Kauravas in the game of gambling. Kauravas were represented by Shakuni (Duryodhana's uncle), who had years of practice on ' Chausar '.Shakuni was well-versed in the game with years of practice and strategy. He was sure Kauravs would win; therefore, he convinced Duryodhana to invite the Pandavas to a game.

Therefore, if a trader has a good strategy and practical experience, stock trading is not gambling; rather, the **stock market is an art!!**

Trading is a game of Probability

Trading must be done keeping some concepts in mind. These are again taken from day-to-day life. A trader must remember that trading is an art, and to excel in this art, they must keep in mind some concepts or principles. These concepts will help him stay disciplined thoroughly.

Before that, let us understand why trading is an art; trading is a game of probability, not gambling.

Did you know that 95% of traders lose money in the stock market, and only 5% make money?

Who are these 5% winners who take the money of the other 95% of traders? 95% of traders are gamblers who trade with emotions and guesswork. The remaining 5% winners are professional traders who trade with specific rules, discipline, and a successful strategy and take money from the other 95% of traders.

Stock trading is an art, but traders often blame their luck. For professional traders, it's simply a game of probability. For a trader or investor, it's the art of reading charts and simple maths.

If any trader can understand the basic principle of demand and supply and increase the probability of winning or losing from 50:50

to 80:20, the chances of winning or making returns from intraday trading can shoot up to 80 to 90%. Therefore, raise your winning probabilities and take the money home.

By now, you must have cleared your doubts and understood the stock market and traders.

Moving ahead, let us start building our knowledge for a better understanding of UDTS© in the next section. The next two chapters are building blocks for understanding UDTS©.

CHAPTER 7
WHY DO WE NEED A TRADING STRATEGY?

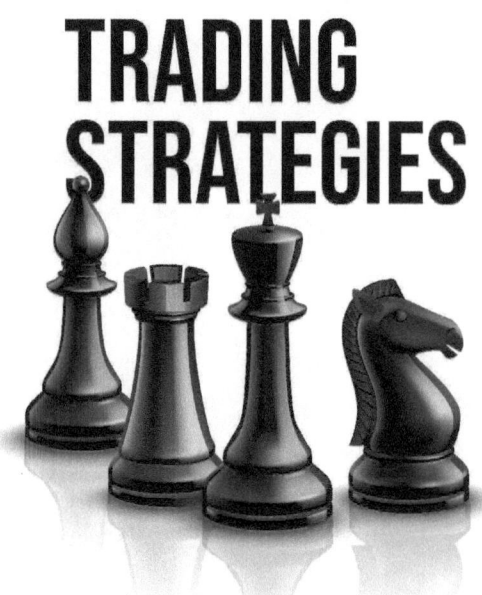

Strategy, in simple words, means: a plan one uses in order to achieve something.

Every day, in every way, traders use different strategies to try and make a profit. Sometimes they succeed, and sometimes they do not. But it's always important to learn from your mistakes, and I always try to find new and better trading methods.

One of the essential things in intraday trading is having a strategy. You need to know what you're doing and why you're doing it. With a robust trading strategy, it's easier to trade, and you will not make mistakes that can cost you a lot of money.

In the real world, several variables can affect a trade's outcome. For example, in the stock market, news events can cause prices to fluctuate rapidly, which makes it challenging to stick to a strict trading strategy. Besides, emotions also play a crucial role in trading. When prices start to move in an unexpected direction, it can be tempting to make impulsive decisions. However, if a trader sticks to their strategy and remains disciplined, they can be successful in the long run.

In my three decades of experience, I've seen two driving forces in how we approach trading:

1. The need to make money
2. The need to protect ourselves from losses

Both are important drivers, but they can sometimes conflict with each other. For example, if we are worried about making money, we may take more risks than we should. On the other hand, if we are concerned about losses, we may not take more risks. The key is to strike a balance between the two forces. We need to take enough chances to make profits, but not to the extent that we expose ourselves to unnecessary losses. This is not always easy, but it is something we constantly need to strive for to be successful traders.

Striking a balance is all about setting goals and aligning objectives with them. When it comes to taking risks, my eyes are always on the horizon for what's coming next, i.e., the latest news, price movements, and market conditions, among others. I weigh all these factors against each other to decide how much risk I'm willing to take, and simultaneously, I am not caught off guard. My suggestion is that you do not have a myopic view while trading. I have tried to create a balance between the above two factors in the strategy we are going to understand in the coming chapters.

TRADING STRATEGY FOR DIFFERENT GOALS

In my career, I have seen all types of traders and know what they can accomplish with their trading goals. I have also seen how some traders make trading seem much more complicated than it is. The best trading strategy will vary depending on the trader's goals, risk tolerance, and other market-related factors. However, some general principles can be followed to make the most of a trading strategy:

- Have a clear and concise plan for implementing the strategy. This plan should outline the entry and exit points for trades and the risk management strategy used. Without a clear plan, it will be challenging to execute the strategy in a disciplined and effective manner.
- Stick to the plan and resist the temptation to stray from it. Many traders make the mistake of deviating from their plan when things are going well, only to see their profits quickly evaporate when the market turns against them.
- Continuously monitor the performance of the strategy and make necessary adjustments. The market is constantly changing and evolving, so a trading strategy that is successful today may not be successful tomorrow. By regularly monitoring the strategy's performance and adjusting as needed, traders can adapt to the ever-changing market conditions and keep their edge.
- Apart from a good strategy, learning about market behaviour—why prices go up and down, what tangible and intangible factors have a bearing on index movements, etc.—is crucial.

CHAPTER

8 NEED FOR A SIMPLE STRATEGY WITHOUT CUMBERSOME TOOLS OF TECHNICAL ANALYSIS

Technical Analysis is cumbersome.

Technical Analysis includes many tools, indicators, charts, and patterns that help understand demand and supply in a Stock or Index. As a result, Technical Analysis supports a trader in making a profitable decision to buy or sell a stock.

But the problem is that traders generally do not know which technical tool or indicator they need to analyse the market. There are more than 35 technical tools and indicators used around the world. Each tool provides an inference on the parameter built, leading to heavy confusion during trading. Moreover, there is a limitation to every technical tool that they give a hypothesis on a specific time frame or interval (default settings).

We must use a multi-time frame interval to get more precise results. So my hunt for an easy way out was on. I was searching for a simple, easy-to-understand strategy that captured the essence of all the technical tools.

I wanted to devise a plan on which people could rely. If my strategy suggested buying a stock, all technical tools should also indicate buying as the best step, and vice versa. I was searching for the **"Mother of All Strategies"** that could give precise results with a simple approach and give the highest probability of winning my trade.

CHAPTER 9
UNI-DIRECTIONAL TRADE STRATEGIES©

Simplistic Trading Strategies for A Common Man - Uni-Directional Trade Strategies© - Best stock trading strategy for intraday and positional trading.

People enter the stock market without gaining formal knowledge, and a lack of professional guidance results in losing money. Stock market traders often lack an understanding of basic demand and supply in the market, and their decision to buy or sell often gets wrong, starting a vicious cycle of losing money and then again trying to earn from the stock market in the next chance. Traders slowly and steadily start gambling and never understand their mistakes, and then they start blaming luck.

But, my dear readers, trading is an art; it's a science of demand and supply coupled with many factors driving the price. No one can precisely predict the market or give a sure-shot call.

In my opinion, a trader can only be strengthened through knowledge. But as per my experience over the last 30 years, people do study and know Technical Analysis, but they lack its applicability in the live market.

Traders always search for a simple way to trade in the live market. Having any software besides them can solve the issue momentarily, but not having any idea at all about how and why the market is moving will always leave traders confused.

IFMC® has designed a simplistic and innovative trading method for stock market beginners and traders to trade accurately and confidently in the stock market. A common man who doesn't know the complexities of stock trading or is a beginner finds it difficult and cumbersome to understand technical analysis tools.

***Uni-directional Trade Strategies* (UDTS©), the world's best trading strategies for Intraday and Positional Trading, are based on basic tools of Line Charts and Candle Charts.**

UDTS© is the best share market trading strategy for beginners, investors, and traders who want to learn how to do intraday, short-positional, positional, long-positional, and wealth creation trading and aspire to become expert traders.

UDTS© Strategies are a set of rules and disciplines I have used and will continue to use in my trading career. Out of all the copy write strategies I have developed, UDTS© is the most popular, as it is simple to understand and requires no cumbersome technical analysis tools. It has now become the strategy of a common trader. It has a high probability of winning and gives the trader an excellent risk-reward ratio.

UDTS© trading strategies teach when to buy, what to buy, and when to sell in the utmost simple manner possible with the help of trend analysis. It gives an understanding of demand and supply from basic to advance.

UDTS© Bunch of 9 Wonderful Trading Strategies, and it's a popular online course of IFMC®. In this book, we are sharing a few strategies based on candles only.

Some salient points of UDTS © strategy are:

1. **Unique Stock Trading Strategies for All Market Segments:** UDTS© strategies apply in all segments of the capital market, futures markets, commodity markets, and currency markets.
2. **Trade with accuracy and confidence:** UDTS© is the only trading strategy that helps traders trade confidently and accurately in the market. After learning UDTS©, one can easily identify the trends. Traders can easily identify the entry and exit points for trades. By simply reading the candle, traders can get the answers to **what to buy, when to buy, when to sell, and what to sell.** By decoding the answers to these questions, traders gain mastery over their trades.

After going through UDTS©, you will gain the ability to generate **your own stock market trading calls**. UDTS© encompasses conventional technical indicators and combines them in a way to provide the most powerful and robust trading strategies.

3. **Highest success ratio:** UDTS© delivers a basic understanding of demand and supply to catch the right trend, which, in turn, helps to precisely find the entry and exit in any given time frame, thus increasing the probability of winning and turning it into a high success ratio.
4. **Emotionless Trading with an Ideal Trading Mechanism:** UDTS© is a mechanism for emotionless trading because we have fixed parameters, i.e., if the charts fulfil all the parameters, you can buy, sell, or exit; however, even if one of the parameters is not fulfilled, the mechanism still allows you to enter or exit. After practising the UDTS© strategies, you can make your own intraday trading calls or tips.
5. **UDTS Strategy is build on common market behaviour:** "Stock Market Moves in a Trend". The strategy took advantage of market behaviour to get precise results.
6. **UDTS© Intraday Trading Strategy is based on a Multi-Frame Time Interval** to get the highest accuracy and success rate. According to the UDTS strategy, traders should consider both long and short-interval trends while taking a trade. This gives a better probability of winning. **Multiple Time Frame Analysis** is a great way to increase your success rate as an intraday trader.
7. **Monetising NIFTY and Sensex Trend:** During intraday trading in stocks, it is important to understand the trend of the index as well. UDTS© advocates that the trend of the index can influence the price of a particular stock. How to monetise index trends in intraday trading will learn in UDTS TRADE MODEL.
8. **Basket Trading:** UDTS© advocates basket trading instead of trading in a single stock. This rule increases the trader's winning probability in his trades. Professional traders never trade in a single stock because they know they are not gambling; they follow the rule of not putting all their eggs in one basket.
9. **Sectoral Analysis:** UDTS© also advocates that traders should buy the stocks of those sectors that are currently in high demand and sell the stocks of sectors that are in high supply. We will understand this point in UDTS© TRADE MODEL.

ACCURACY OF UDTS© STRATEGY

"**Trust, But Verify**" - Ronald Reagan (40th President of the United States)

The phrase became internationally known in English after Suzanne Massie, an American scholar, taught it to Ronald Reagan, the then-president of the United States, the latter of whom used it on several occasions in the context of nuclear disarmament discussions with the Soviet Union. The quote means, *"I hear what you are saying, but I'll trust you only after verification."* Indeed, the sage advice applies to all traders. Unfortunately, there is potential for fraud and deception in the trading world. To protect yourself, constantly verifying the information you are given is crucial. If something sounds too good to be true, it probably is. Please do your research, and never take someone's word without verifying it yourself. This can help you avoid being scammed or taken advantage of in the world of trading.

Many traders believe picking by a zero-commission broker, free-to-use tools, or the following referral is easy to make trading tips. However, what the traders do not understand are the challenges associated with it. Making money in the stock market is complex. New traders should not jump into the market with both feet but should verify each step of the plan as it is being implemented. Google provides information on virtually any subject. Ignore the advertisements.

Use a small amount of money as you begin trading or start paper trading to verify whether any strategy is profitable.

After going through the book and understanding the strategy, you must start with paper trading. Paper trading means simulating trades in the live market without investing any money. It is a great way to test the strategy and determine its effectiveness before risking any capital. If the strategy is successful in paper trading, you can continue live trading with real money.

It is a very powerful strategy that can help you make huge profits in the long run. However, it is essential to remember that you will not always be successful with every trade. There will be times when you lose money. But if you stick with the strategy and keep making baskets of trades, you will eventually see the success you are looking for.

CHAPTER

10

UDTS© - A SKILL FOR MONETISING MARKET BEHAVIOUR

With a very simple and interesting example, let us understand the concept of Market Behaviour. The market moves in trend (monthly, weekly, or daily). This example will help you understand UDTS© very easily. Therefore, please read it carefully to get the skills to monetise market behaviour in your strategy.

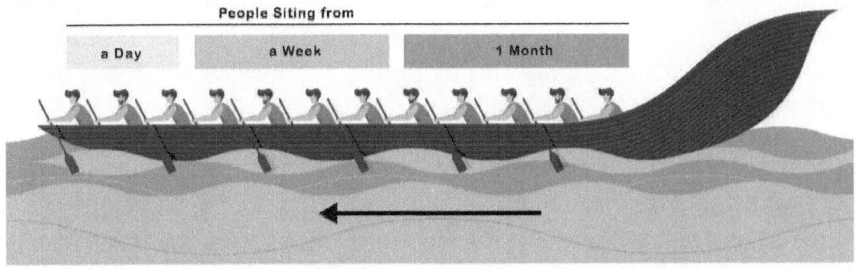

People sitting for a month, week, and day are rowing in the same direction

In this example, the boat is a stock, and the passengers are traders. Let us assume that there is a huge boat sailing in the river with many people in it for the last month, and they all are rowing forward, so the boat will go forward.

The boat stops, and some new people board it, and they, too, start rowing it for another week. As a result, the boat starts moving at a better pace.

Now the boat stops again, and some new passengers come aboard; they also row it. So, now what's happening is that the ones sitting in the boat for the past month and week and those who entered a day before are also rowing it.

The boat will move faster because all the passengers are rowing it. This is exactly what happens in bullish stocks, where monthly, weekly, and daily trends are all in an upward move.

Now let us assume another scenario: passengers who boarded a day before started rowing backwards, while those who've been there for a week or a month are still rowing forward.

Now the speed will be slightly slower because some people are rowing backwards. After seeing these people rowing backwards, those sitting for one week also started rowing backwards, and those sitting for the last month also started rowing backwards. The net result will be the boat making a U-turn and starting to go backwards.

The stock market is like a big boat, i.e., there are many people on the boat, just as there are many stocks in the market. And just like some people on the boat are moving forward, others are moving backwards. Some stocks are also moving up, while others are moving down. The stocks moving up are taking the market forward, while the ones moving down are taking it backward.

The stock market is like a boat, i.e., it can't take a turn immediately. It will take some time to change. So, a trader must keep a sharp eye on the market. This example of market behaviour forms the basis of our UDTS© strategy. The stock market is all about demand and supply.

If there is a higher demand for a stock, the price will go up, and if there is lower demand, the price will go down.

By the above illustration, you all must have understood that markets have particular behaviour to move in a trend. And we will try to monetise this market behaviour in our strategy.

CHAPTER 11
DIFFERENT TRADING STYLES

Traders can use different trading styles depending on their goals and preferences. Two of the most common types are intraday and positional trading.

Intraday trading involves taking trades that last for only one day. Traders who use this style usually look to take advantage of small price movements in the market. They typically close their positions before the end of the day, so they do not have to worry about overnight risks.

On the other hand, positional trading involves holding trades for a longer period of time, sometimes for weeks or even months. Traders who use this style are usually more interested in catching more significant price movements in the market. As a result, they are willing to hold on to their positions for more extended periods, even if it means incurring some overnight risks.

Each style has its advantages and disadvantages. Intraday trading is generally considered riskier as positions are held for a shorter period of time, and there is more potential for things to go wrong. However, it can also be more lucrative as traders can take advantage of short-term market movements. On the other hand, positional trading is generally considered less risky as positions are held for longer, giving the market more time to move in the trader's favour. However, it can also be less profitable as there is less potential for short-term market movements.

The best trading style depends on the trader's goals, risk tolerance, and type. For example, some traders may prefer the quick-paced action of intraday trading. In contrast, others may prefer the more measured approach of positional trading. Ultimately, it is up to the trader to decide which style is best for them.

Now, let us discuss each style of trading in depth.

INTRADAY TRADING

Intraday trading is the buying and selling of securities within the same day. This type of trading differs from other types of trading, such as swing trading or long-term investing, which involve holding securities for extended periods. Intraday trading is a game of forecasting the next 3-5 Hrs of a stock which is easier to predict a longer move.

There are several reasons why someone might choose to engage in intraday trading.

1. Intraday trading can provide a way to make more money quicker than other types of trading because the intraday trader can take advantage of the fluctuating stock prices within a day.
2. It can help you limit your losses. This is because you can exit the trade with smaller stop losses within a day.
3. In intraday trading, traders get higher leverage from brokers through margin limits. This way, traders can trade 5 to 8 times higher on their capital. However, it is always advisable to stay within your boundaries and not go over-bought with the borrowed money, as sometimes external factors can also shake the technical analysis, though for a short term and if the positions are over-leveraged, then you can invite troubles.

Intraday trading is a popular strategy where traders attempt to capitalise on short-term price movements in the market. This type of trading can be risky, as prices can move quickly and unpredictably. However, with a well-planned strategy, traders can minimise risks and maximise their chances of success.

Your strategy should consider the time of day, market conditions, and the assets you're trading. It will be best if you also have the plan to manage your risk, including how to exit a losing trade.

With a solid strategy, you can trade confidently, knowing you have the plan to make consistent profits.

There are several reasons why intraday trading is difficult. For example:

Firstly, intraday traders need to be able to read and interpret market data quickly and accurately, which can be challenging, particularly for those new to the markets.

Secondly, intraday trading requires discipline and focus. Traders need to stick to their trading plan and not get distracted by the market's noise.

Finally, intraday trading can be stressful. The markets are constantly moving, and there is always the risk of losing money.

You need to be able to focus for the entire time frame between 9am to 3.30pm. It can be tough for many people as the markets can be very volatile, and there is a lot of information to process. Additionally, you need to have a good understanding of the market and be able to make split-second decisions.

Here are some more interesting and important points you need to understand as an intraday trader:

1. **Intraday is a product of brokers:** Intraday pushes sales and volumes in the market. Brokers get brokerages on every buy and sell. Thus, it is beneficial to the broker more than it is to a trader. The broker also provides leverage to the traders so that trading intraday is lucrative for the trader because he can buy or sell more than his capacity. Thus, the trader must opt for quality trades rather than quantity trades.
2. **Intraday trading is addictive:** Traders get addicted and often end up harming themselves. It's natural because, sometimes, the market conditions are too favourable, and traders get unexpected returns, thus making the trader greedier and prompting him to take more risks.
3. **Intraday trading has a wide range:** Traders can make intraday in equity, commodity, derivatives, and currency markets. Here, traders get a chance to sell first and buy later, thus making

intraday all the more lucrative. So a trader must weigh the financial instruments he wishes to use and know them in advance.
4. **Intraday trading is a game of correctly forecasting the next** 2-3 hours of trend. The trader can win the game if he achieves it.

Having understood intraday trading, let's now understand the difference between intraday and positional trading.

POSITIONAL TRADING

Positional trading is a trading style in which we take our positions for more than a day. For example, if I purchase a stock today, and I'm not selling it today but tomorrow or maybe after some days.

We can do positional trading in the following segments: the capital market (only the buying side), commodity markets, derivative markets, and currency markets. But in the capital market, we can only take the buying side positions in positional trades; we cannot carry sell positions to the next days. Due to this restriction from the stock exchange, traders use derivatives to create sell positions for longer periods.

If you have taken a sell position in the capital market, you have to buy it back or cover it on the same day. But if you want to take a buy position, then the capital market allows you to take delivery, pay full price, and sell it after two or three days or whenever you want to sell it.

Position trading involves taking a long-term view of the market and holding a position for an extended period. Position traders typically only trade a few times. Still, they usually look for significant, trend-based moves when they do trade. This type of trading can be very profitable if done correctly, but it can also be risky. Therefore, position traders must be very patient and have a strong understanding of market trends to be successful.

Positional trading is further divided into two types:
- **Swing Trading:** Swing trading is a short to medium-term positional trading style in which a trader can close his trades for some days or weeks.

- **Long-term Positional Trading:** Long-term positional trading is for a longer duration in which a trader carries his positions for months or years.

SWING TRADING

Swing traders seek opportunities in a stock's short-term price swing in the overall trend of the stock's price. For example, while a stock may continue to rise over the next six months, there will be quick drops in the price for a few days or weeks before it rebounds and continues its trend. This is where swing traders see their opportunity; they can get in at the bottom of that dip and ride it back up for a few days or even a few weeks before it dips again.

This is the beauty of swing trading. While you do not earn profits quite as quickly as day trading, you can complete a few weekly trades to earn an income. But it requires far less time commitment than other styles, making it an excellent choice for those looking for supplemental income that won't interfere with their job.

LONG POSITION TRADING

You learned that the main difference between these strategies is the holding period. The holding period of swing trading is concise, i.e., sometimes a few days or, at most, a few weeks. And while position traders do not maintain positions for years (or a lifetime) as investors do, they hold positions much longer than swing traders. Sometimes, position trading entails having a position for weeks to months.

This means you won't pay much mind to daily noise; instead, you will look at long-term outcomes. An excellent way to think about position trading is a happy medium between swing trading and long-term investing. You can use position trading as a means of preparing for your future. However, one key difference between position trading and long-term investing is that position traders may go either short or long on their position. Investors, on the other hand, always go long.

With position trading, you spend even less time in front of a screen than swing traders, making it an excellent approach for those who have a full-time job and can't afford to spend an hour or two watching charts daily.

Now that you understand these two trading styles better, the question is which style suits you the best. Keep in mind—there is no right answer. You do not necessarily have to choose just one or the other. Instead, you can create a well-rounded trading strategy using both styles simultaneously.

WHAT ARE THE CRITICAL DIFFERENCES BETWEEN INTRADAY AND POSITIONAL TRADING?

The most crucial difference is that intraday traders typically do not hold onto their positions overnight, while positional traders do. Intraday traders are more exposed to short-term price fluctuations and are more likely to experience losses if the market moves against them. Positional traders, on the other hand, can afford to take a more patient approach and wait for the market to move in their favour.

Another key difference is that intraday trading generally requires a higher risk tolerance and capital level than positional trading. Because intraday traders are often leveraged and are more exposed to losses if the market moves against them, positional traders, on the other hand, can afford to be more conservative with their capital and take a longer-term view.

Finally, intraday trading is generally more suited to active, experienced traders. In contrast, positional trading can be a good strategy for beginners and professional investors. So, consider a positional trading strategy if you're new to the markets.

Ultimately, the best way to choose between intraday and positional trading is to experiment with both approaches and see which suits your personality and is aligned with your risk tolerance appetite.

Let us understand this with an example:

Intraday trading is like driving a car in a crowded market.

If you are driving a car in a crowded market, you encounter many obstructions. There is always a chance that your car may get scratched because of heavy traffic, so you go with the utmost safety and mental alertness, using all your tools—rear view, side view mirrors, clutch, accelerator, brakes, etc., and only experts can do that. Intraday trading is similar to driving in a crowded place as it requires quick decisions in a fraction of time and with full mental alertness.

Positional trading is like driving a car on a highway.

If you drive a car on the highway, there are fewer obstructions and a lesser chance of your car getting scratched. An average driver can do it. He has enough time to check and use all the previously mentioned tools, which a driver in a crowded place does not. That is positional trading. That's why we say positional trading is better for beginners or traders with idle time and patience.

DIFFERENCE BETWEEN INTRADAY, SHORT-TERM POSITIONAL (SWING), MEDIUM-TERM POSITIONAL (SWING), AND LONG-TERM POSITIONAL TRADING

Time Frame And Volatility Difference Between Different Trading Styles
Intraday is performed in cash market / future / option / currency / commodities – Time frame – One day – Volatility – Trends in intraday can change 2 to 3 times
Short-Term Positional can be done in the cash market (only buying side)/future/option/currency/commodities – Time frame – 2 days to 5 days – Volatility – Trends can change 2 to 3 times a week
Medium Term Positional trading can be done in the cash market (only buying side)/future/option/currency/commodities – Time frame – 5 days to 15 days – Volatility – Trends can change 2 to 3 times a month
Long-Term Positional trading can be done in the cash market (only buying side)/future/option/currency/commodities – Time frame – 1 month to 4 months – Volatility – Trends can change 2 to 3 times in 6 months

Intraday – for one-day trading: It is highly volatile, needs much concentration and mental alertness, small stop-losses and small targets, compulsory trade square-offs on the same day, and it can be done in the capital markets, commodities, derivatives, and currencies.

Short-Term Positional – for 2 to 5-day trading: It is less volatile than intraday, manageable even applying low concentration and bigger stop losses and bigger targets than intraday, and it can be done in the capital market (only buying side trades), commodities, derivatives, and currencies.

Medium-Term Positional Trading – for 5 to 15-day trading: It is less volatile, needs lesser concentration, and has bigger stop-losses and targets than short-term positional trading, and it can be done in the capital market (only buying side trades), commodities, derivatives, and currencies.

Long-Term Positional Trading – Usually, the term is 1 to 4 months: It is less volatile, needs less concentration, and has bigger stop-losses and targets than positional term trading, and it can be done in the capital market (only buying side trades), commodities, derivatives, and currencies.

After understanding the different trading styles, let us move to different time frame charts for different trading styles. Yes, according to the trading interval, traders use different time frame charts.

CHAPTER 12
DIFFERENT TIME FRAME CHARTS FOR TRADING

Different time frame charts for trading can provide different levels of detail and allow traders to make different decisions. The charts are extremely helpful in making informed decisions about when to enter and exit a trade. For example, a long-term chart may show overall trends, while a short-term chart may show more detailed price action.

Some traders may use multiple time frame charts to get a complete market picture. For example, a trader may look at a long-term chart to identify a trend and then use a short-term chart to time their entry into the market.

Different time frame charts can be used for different purposes, so it is up to the trader to decide which time frame or frames are most appropriate for their trading style and goals.

On monthly time frame charts, you are looking at a larger time frame and trying to catch the trend, demand, and supply at intervals of 30 to 60 days. This gives you a better idea of where the market is going and what you can expect. You can also use this time frame to set your trading goals and objectives. By looking at the monthly chart, you can get a sense of the market's overall direction and identify potential areas of support and resistance.

On weekly charts, you notice the direction every 10 to 15 days. By looking at the weekly chart, you can identify weekly trends and patterns that you may not be able to see on the monthly chart.

You can identify short-term trends and patterns in the daily time frame. However, on the intraday charts, we can see very short-term trends on hourly, 15 min, and 5 min charts to identify the present stock trend.

It is important to choose the right time frame charts for intraday trading.

RIGHT TIME-FRAME CHARTS FOR INTRADAY TRADING?

Regarding intraday trading, using the best time frames will help increase your probability of winning because it allows you to make more informed decisions. If you're looking at a daily chart or intraday charts only and trying to make trade decisions based on that, you're not going to be as successful as someone who is also looking at a weekly or monthly chart.

This means you should not only look at a single time frame chart but use multiple time frames in your analysis. We will cover that shortly. For now, know that using the best time frames is crucial if you want to be successful in intraday trading.

UDTS© advocates multiple time frames, i.e., monthly, weekly, daily, hourly, and even 15-minute time frame charts, to get the best results.

Using multiple time frames in your analysis helps you better understand the market. For example, you might look at a daily chart to find trends and identify support and resistance levels, but then use a fifteen-minute chart to time your entries and exits. It is called **Multiple Time Frame Analysis,** and it is a great way to increase your success rate as an intraday trader.

UDTS© intraday strategy is based on a multi-frame time interval to get the highest accuracy and success rate. According to UDTS© principles, if a stock is bullish on bigger interval time frame charts, it has to be bullish on smaller time frame charts also to take a buy position in that stock. That means the stock can either be bullish or bearish on any given trading day. It can't be both.

For example, if a stock is bullish on bigger intervals charts (monthly, weekly, and daily), then the trader has to find only bullish opportunities in intraday (when smaller intervals 45 min and 15 min charts show bullish).

CONFIDENT TRADERS ARE EITHER BULLS OR BEARS ON A PARTICULAR DAY.

Suppose a stock is bullish on bigger intervals. In that case, you must take only the buying side position if the intraday time frame is also bullish or vice versa. I often see traders change their views while trading intraday, which shows their weak confidence.

Let me tell you one humorous line that was said to me by my senior during my ring trading experience. You must have heard about the two frequently used terms of the stock market—Bull and Bear. Both make money with the right strategy.

Now you will ask me, "If both make money, who are the losers?"

Yes, there is one more term that I'm sure you must not have heard about, i.e., The Pig.

Pigs are generally greedy, always fearful, and meant for slaughter.

Such traders are not much confident in their trades; they keep on shuffling between bullish and bearish trades in intraday trading. Both bulls and bears take all the money from these pigs due to their fearful and greedy nature.

Both Bulls and Bears are confident traders—they know when to enter or exit a trade—but pigs are under-confident—they are fearful of losing money and keep on changing their thoughts of being bull or bear, resulting in losses. A trader can't be both bull or bear at the same time or same day in any particular stock. By doing so, he can decrease his winning probabilities. So if a trader is bullish on a particular stock on any particular day, he should always try to catch buying opportunities only.

PART B

ANALYTICS OF UNI-DIRECTIONAL TRADE STRATEGIES©

CHAPTER 13

HOW TO MAKE THE VIEW FROM FUNDAMENTALS?

BULLISH OR BEARISH VIEW

The first and most crucial step to start trading is to create a view. It means a trader must know whether the trade is bullish (you want to buy a stock) or bearish (you want to sell a stock) on a particular stock. There are two schools of thought for making the view—fundamental analysis and technical analysis.

A fundamental analyst will look at factors affecting the price in the long term, such as earnings reports, economic data, company news and analysis, and other financial reports. Thus, this study is much needed for long-term investors as this data does not significantly affect the short-term; typically, long-term investors use this study to make a long-term outlook or view.

A technical analysis, on the other hand, studies demand and supply. Analysts look for technical parameters like charts, support, resistance levels, moving averages, and other technical indicators to find patterns indicating where the stock is heading for trading in the short term. Usually, traders use this study to form a short-term outlook or view.

Let us understand with an example to understand it better. Let us assume I am in a new city and want to dine at a restaurant. Upon going, I saw many restaurants lined up. So, to find the best, I conduct a quick analysis because I do not have time to check many restaurants, and I am really hungry.

I am searching for overall hygiene and tasty food at a reasonable price. One way could be to go and check each restaurant's food and cooking methods, the raw ingredients they are using, the chef, the hygiene level, and the set prices for the food. Then, after doing all this research, I would probably come to a conclusion about selecting the best one in the market.

But such research is helpful if I have to do some kind of long-term business with them.

For a shorter-term goal, i.e., to have a quick bite, I do not need to do such a long analysis. Rather, quick check parameters would help me meet my goal of selecting a good restaurant. I would check on the restaurants attracting more crowds, minimal waiting, and reasonable prices. Thus, selecting a restaurant would be easier because my goal is clear, and my parameters are set. We need to do this while selecting the stocks for trading.

With the above 2 ways, I have tried to clarify the difference between fundamental and technical approaches.

As per the UDTS© principle, we advocate using fundamental and technical analysis to get a complete picture of the market and make informed trading decisions to achieve the highest probability of winning. Therefore, to trade like a professional, you must consider both fundamental and technical parameters to achieve your trading goals.

Here are a few steps you need to follow:

1. Making a view using Fundamental Analysis
2. Making a view using Technical Analysis

Making a view using Fundamental Analysis has two parts:

1. **Company analysis:** This covers the detailed financial analysis of a stock, such as its EPS, profits, ratios, balance sheets, etc., which do not change frequently or in a short time, so, as a trader, it does not have any significant weightage in making a short-term view for a particular stock or sector.
2. **News and data analysis:** This has a big weightage for traders in the short term as every news or data directly affects the stock price. So, one must fully understand the news and data and their effect on a particular sector or stock.

For intraday trading, the news carries more weight. Let us understand the impact of news on stock movements:

We that there was a global lockdown in March 2020 due to a pandemic. People were locked in their houses and were doing work from home. Experienced traders made their fortunes from sectors and stocks in entertainment, pharma, telecom, and NIFTY. Everything was at a standstill, but these sectors had a huge demand.

Let us see this situation from a trader's perspective; only then can we hear the voice of the stock market from the right perspective. And the moment you understand this, you understand the market. If you learn the language of the market, it will tell you everything you want to know.

1. During the lockdown, all people across ages were glued to either TV or the internet for entertainment and education. If you see the charts between March and September 2020, stocks of entertainment and telecom saw a massive surge.
2. Another industry that experienced high growth during the pandemic was pharma. Due to an increased need for life-saving drugs, vaccines, medical equipment, gloves, sanitisers, and masks, among others. These companies worked tirelessly to develop a vaccine to protect us from this potentially deadly virus.

From news of day-to-day life, traders try to infer the effect on the stock market and stocks. For this, traders must learn how to understand the news.

Analysing the news is an important skill for any trader. It means identifying the main points of a story and understanding the implications of what is being reported. In addition, with an understanding of news, traders can analyse and profit from it.

DATA ANALYSIS

Data plays an important role in deciphering how the economy is faring and what stocks will be impacted. For example, let us look at the GDP, oil inventory, and inflation data. We can get a good idea of how different sectors will be impacted.

Let me elaborate; if the **GDP** rises, certain sectors will likely do as well. However, if the oil inventory increases, it can negatively impact the oil sector stocks. Thus, it's essential to understand the data and how it will affect different sectors before making investment decisions.

Similarly, if **oil prices** fluctuate, it will either benefit or harm oil manufacturing companies (ONGC, BPCL, HPCL, etc.). If oil prices fall, the ONGC will help because they can buy their raw material at a lower price. However, if oil prices rise, the ONGCs will be harmed because they will have to buy their raw material at a higher price. These few market factors are interconnected. We need to understand these things to make informed decisions about investing in the stock market.

Another important factor is **inflation,** which affects the stock market. When inflation is high, the prices of goods and services increase, leading to lower profits for companies and less money available for investors to buy stocks. In addition, high inflation can lead to higher interest rates, making it more expensive for companies to borrow money, leading to lower stock prices.

Monetary policy is also an essential factor affecting the stock market. When the Federal Reserve/RBI raises interest rates, it can lead to lower stock prices because companies are more expensive to borrow money. In addition, higher interest rates can lead to a stronger dollar, making it more difficult for companies that export goods to sell their products overseas.

Government, central government, and central banks decide to keep the inflation within a specifically targeted range. Thus, the Central Bank is always trying to keep the economy stable, and inflation controlled. They do this by changing interest rates. These changes can have a significant impact on the market price.

Apart from economic indicators like inflation and interest rates, political events can also affect the markets. In addition, other factors like budget announcements, elections, and monetary policy also have a substantial impact.

To understand the market or forecast market movements, we must look at the underlying factors driving those movements to raise our winning probabilities in our trades.

Chapter 13: How to make the view from fundamentals? | 57

Live Market Examples on News Analysis

Crude oil monthly chart

HPCL July 2017 monthly chart

Let us compare the charts of crude oil and Hindustan petroleum. We all know that if crude oil prices rise, oil manufacturing companies will suffer losses because their margins will shrink as they will have to buy costlier crude, but they will not be able to sell the end consumer product at higher prices because of government restrictions.

Previously, the OMCs could not increase the price in the same proportion. But now, after a policy change, if crude oil prices rise, oil manufacturing companies can also increase the price of the end consumer product.

Let us compare the charts of crude oil and one of the ONGC, i.e., HPCL, between July 2017 and Sep 2018, when crude was controlled by the government. Here, crude started rising from July 2017 until Sep 2018; at the same time, HPCL started falling in the same period.

NIFTY monthly chart

Chapter 13: How to make the view from fundamentals? | 59

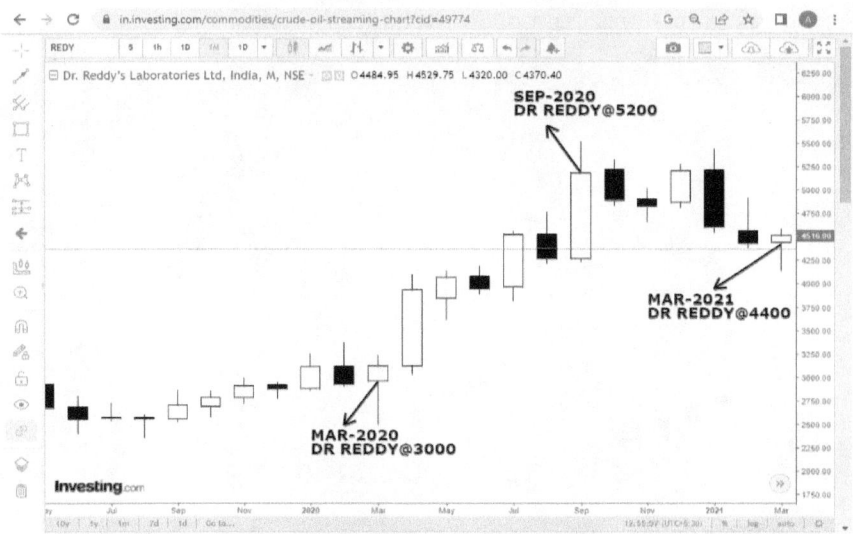

Dr. Reddy's Lab monthly chart

Let us take one more example to understand it better. Here I have taken Dr. Reddy's Lab and NIFTY charts for comparison. You may take any other pharma company to see the pattern.

In March 2020, during the COVID lockdown, the market dipped as low as 8500. People were getting sick, and the expense of medications was increasing.

It was very clear that demand in pharmaceutical companies was high, and their profits were also on the rise due to the high consumption of medicines and other pharma products. Charts of Dr. Reddy's Lab reflect a sharp upward rise from ₹2900 to ₹5200 between March 2020 and Sep 2020.

Let us take one more example of Reliance Industries

RELIANCE INDUSTRIES MONTHLY CHART

In March 2020, when NIFTY was around ₹8,005, Reliance was at ₹1100. All the telecom companies were going to make good profits because most people were working at home and using a lot of data and internet services. The price of Reliance rose to ₹2,400 in just six months.

Glenmark Pharma monthly chart

Chapter 13: How to make the view from fundamentals? | 61

See Glenmark Pharma's chart. It was ₹200 in March 2020, and it rose to ₹550 by Dec 2020. By now, you must have understood how news analysis plays a significant part in making an informed decision.

Let me give you an example of data analysis by comparing the NIFTY and L&T charts.

Larsen & Toubro monthly chart

NIFTY monthly chart

In Feb 2021, the budget advantage was given to the infrastructure sector. L&T's being a top company in the infrastructure sector benefitted the most. After the budget, its price rose from ₹1345 to ₹1593 in just a month.

You must know that news and data analysis are crucial to a trader's decision-making when selecting a stock.

In the next chapter, we will understand how to make a view based on technical parameters.

CHAPTER 14
MAKING TRADING VIEW WITH TREND ANALYSIS

Understanding Candle Charts and how to Analyse Trends

Having understood how to create a view bullish or bearish by news and data analysis, traders must check the stock's technical parameters for trading decisions.

If the trading view with news analysis matches technical parameters, there is a higher chance of success. For example, let us say there is news that crude prices have fallen, and all the related sectors will have a significant impact. If I want to trade in stocks of paints, I will check the technical parameters of those stocks. Let us say I want to compare Asian paints and Berger paints. I feel Berger paint is going to rise, but technical parameters show more demand for Asian Paints than Berger paint, so an intraday trader must choose Asian Paint.

It is the first step in raising our winning probabilities. Now the question is how to read charts and identify demand and supply.

WHAT IS A CANDLE & HOW DO YOU READ CANDLES?

Candlestick charts originated in Japan in the 1700s, when a Japanese man named Homma discovered that, while there was a link between price and the demand and supply of rice, the markets are strongly influenced by the emotions of a trader.

Candle charts are easier to read and clearly indicate demand and supply along with market sentiments.

Each candlestick shows four parameters- High Price, Low Price, Opening Price, and Closing Price of a security and its colour for a specific period. The following colours distinguish the candlesticks (Refer to Figure-1).

White Candlesticks or Green Candlesticks: **Indicate an uptrend. It's a bullish candle.** Black Candlesticks or Red Candlesticks: **Indicate a downtrend. It's a bearish candle**

The candle has two parts: body and shadow (Fig 1)

1. **Body**

The hollow or the filled portion of the candlestick is called the body of the candlestick.

- Long Body - Indicates heavy trading in one direction and strong buying or selling pressure.
- Small Body - Indicates lighter trading or little buying or selling activity.

2. **Shadow**

The long thin lines above and below the body are called the shadow of the candlestick.

- **Upper Shadow** - High is marked by the topmost part of the upper shadow(it's the highest price touched in any given time frame, monthly, weekly, daily, whatever time frame chart the trader is viewing).
- **Lower Shadow** - Low shadow is marked by the bottom part of the lower shadow (it's the lowest price touched in any given time frame, i.e., monthly, weekly, or daily, or whatever time frame the chart a trader is viewing).

Candlestick charts can be seen on different time frames such as monthly, weekly, daily, hourly and even minutes. So by just looking at a candle, one can know the overall health of a stock at any interval.

Time frames represent the duration of candlestick or line charts. For example, looking at a daily chart, each candlestick will represent one day of trading action. If you're looking at a weekly chart, each candlestick will represent one week of trading activity. There are also monthly and yearly time frames.

When we say "white" candle, we mean it is bullish. It is because the opening price is lower than the closing price, indicating that the market is rising. The shadow at the top represents the highest point

Chapter 14: Making Trading View with Trend Analysis | 65

reached during this period, while the shadow at the bottom represents the lowest point. (fig 1)

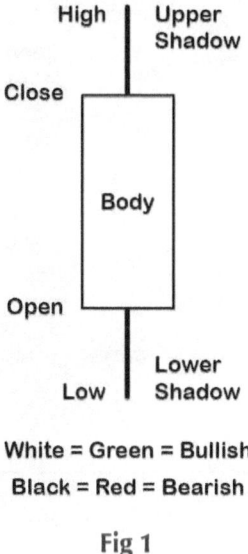

White = Green = Bullish
Black = Red = Bearish

Fig 1

In a vice-versa scenario, if the candle is black, it is a bearish candle. Its opening price is higher than the closing price. (refer to the pic below Figure 2)

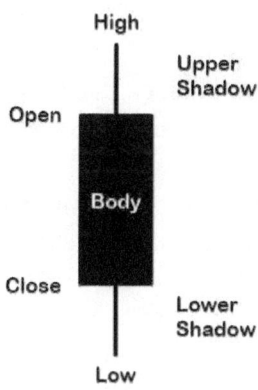

Black = Red = Bearish

Figure 2

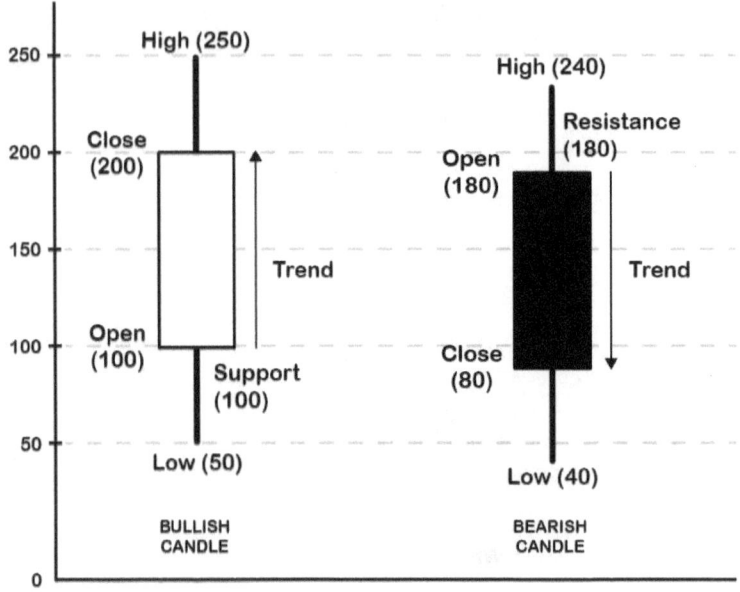

Figure 3

By viewing a candle, you can tell how the stock performs on any particular day. Let us say the stock ABC (Figure. 3) has an opening price of ₹100 and closing at ₹200, with a high of ₹250 and a low of ₹50. You know it's a white candle. Thus just by viewing the candle's colour, you know that the sentiments are bullish. The stock ABC closed above its open price.

In the vice versa scenario, the black candle shows that stock ABC has fallen. In black candles, the opening price is ₹180, and the closing price is ₹80. The stock touched a low of ₹40 and a high of ₹220. In the black candle, the closing price is below the open price. We can easily understand by viewing the black candle that the stock ABC opened at ₹180 and closed at ₹80, making an intraday high of ₹220 and a low of ₹40. (Figure 3)

Hopefully, you must have understood white and black candles and how easy it is to learn about the stock movement by observing them. Keep this understanding in its entirety as we proceed forward, as we will build up more on this knowledge to understand the UDTS© strategy.

WHAT IS A TREND, AND HOW TO VIEW TRENDS ON CANDLES?

A trend is the direction of the market; it can be bearish (falling prices) or bullish (rising prices). Past market patterns reveal that asset prices follow a trend where if the market is bullish, the prices keep rising shortly.

Trend Trading is how traders attempt to realize profits based on the current market trend and the asset's momentum.

We will understand how to view trends as per the UDTS© technique using candles in this section. Before we start, I know many people have already studied or are studying trend analysis differently. It is because there are many different ways to analyse Technical data, just like how different doctors have different ways of diagnosing.

Similarly, different traders view the trend on candles differently. So let us start afresh for a better and clear understanding of the trend as per UDTS©.

We will cover this topic with many examples so that you can understand how to find the perfect trend. If you are on the right trend, there is no need to chase profits; instead, profits will chase you. Still, if you are in the wrong trend, no one can save you from stock trading losses, especially intraday trading. Let us understand the trend.

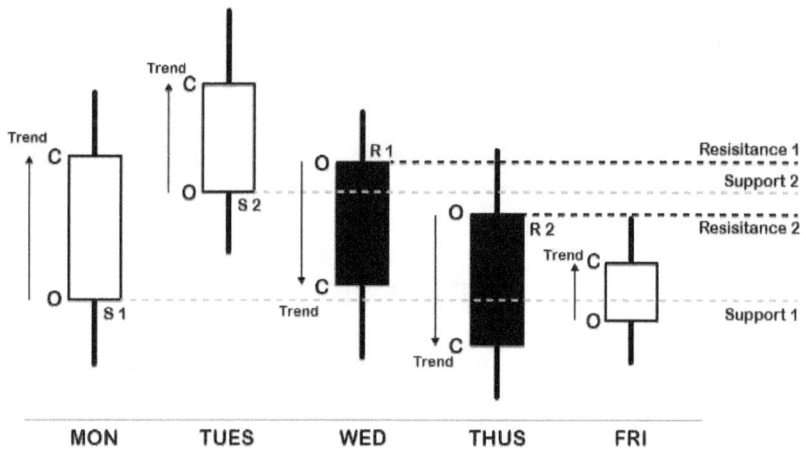

Figure 4

In Figure 3, the first candle formed on Monday is white, clearly showing that the stock opened at a lower price and closed on the higher side, i.e., an uptrend with support of S 1.

Support is the price from where the uptrend started.

The next day is Tuesday; another white candle formed, showing a bullish trend again, and now the support S1 trailed to S2, considered a new support after S1 on Tuesday.

On Wednesday, a black candle is formed, closed below the opening(S2) of the previous white candle (Tuesday candle). The trend is reversed on the daily charts because the bear (black) candle breached the support (S2) and closed that point below. Now on Wednesday's closing, the trend is downward with the resistance of R1.

Resistance is just the opposite of support. It is the price from where the downtrend started.

On Thursday, a black candle was formed again, which means a bear trend with new resistance of R2.

On Friday, a white candle is formed but cannot close above the opening of the previous black candle, R2 (Thursday candle). It means the bulls returned on Friday but could not overpower the bears. Finally, Friday closed with a bear trend.

Monthly Trend

A monthly trend is a complete month that reveals the trend of a stock over an interval of 30 to 60 days. If the trend is bullish on the charts, the stock has had cumulative demand for the last 30 to 60 days.

If there is a demand, there has to be a support price, indicating the point from which demand has been created. If stocks breach this support price, the trend is reversed from bullish to bearish. In a vice-versa scenario, if the monthly trend is bearish, there has to be a resistance point. If the price moves above the resistance level, the monthly trend changes from bearish to bullish.

Check the chart below for an example:

The monthly chart of NIFTY shows a trend with support and resistance levels.

Weekly Trend

A weekly trend is a complete week that reveals the trend of stock throughout 7 to 14 days. If the trend is bullish on the charts, the stock has had cumulative demand for the last 7 to 14 days. If there is a demand, there has to be a support price, indicating the point from which the demand has been created. If stocks breach this support price, the trend is reversed from bullish to bearish.

In a vice-versa scenario, if the weekly trend is bearish, there has to be a resistance point. If the price moves above the resistance level, the weekly trend changes from bearish to bullish.

Check the chart below for example:

NIFTY Weekly Chart

Above is the NIFTY weekly chart; the initial weekly trend is downward, but as the white candle closes above, the resistance of the black candle (17156) trend was changed, and from there, there is a continuous uptrend for the next 11 weeks. The last candle represents the current week, which has an upward trend with a weekly support of 18392.

Daily Trend

A daily trend is the trend of a complete day that reveals a day trend of a stock. If the trend is bullish on the charts, it means the stock has had a cumulative demand on daily charts.

If there is a demand, there has to be a support price, indicating the point from which the demand has been created. If stocks breach this support price, it indicates a reversal of the trend from bullish to bearish.

In a vice-versa scenario, if the daily trend is bearish, there has to be a resistance point. If the price moves above the resistance level, it means the daily trend is changing from bearish to bullish.

Check the chart below for example:

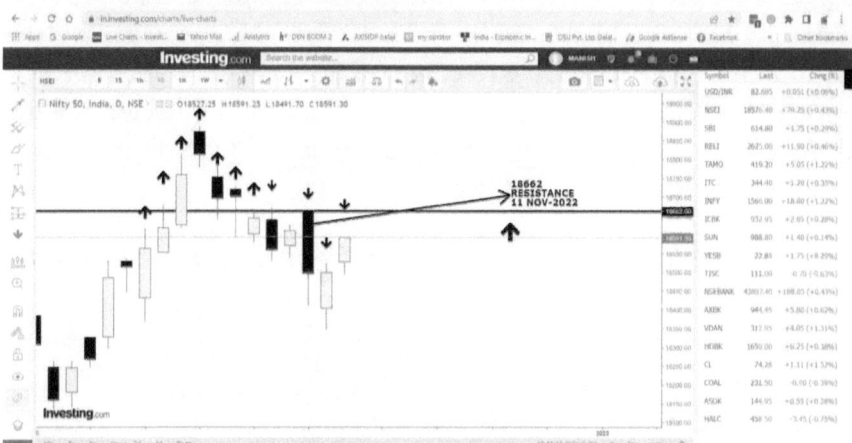

NIFTY DAILY CHART

Above is the NIFTY daily chart. Here, the current daily trend is downward with the resistance of the last black candle open price (18662). If the current price moves above this level, the daily trend is reversed from bearish to bullish. Now, understanding the trend on monthly, weekly, and daily charts, let us move to some live market examples.

Examples to understand trends in candles

Here is the NIFTY daily chart in the image below. You can also open charts on your device for the same period.

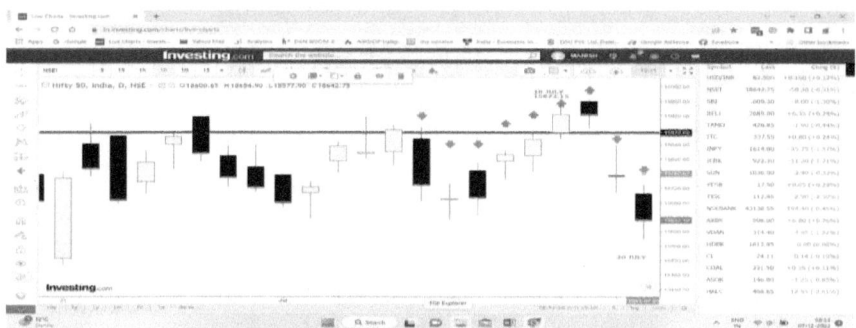

NIFTY Daily Trend

Just watch the last candle of 20 July 2021, which is the current date candle. And before that, there is a small black candle, and before that, there is one more black candle from 18 July. Now, to identify the trend in this image, we have to compare the current candle (20 July) with the previous white candle. The 20 July candle is close below the open price of the last fourth white candle (17 July) on the charts. Thus, the current daily trend is down.

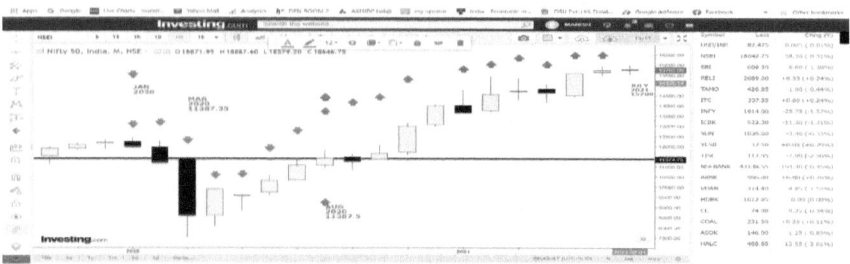

NIFTY Monthly Trend

Let us take one more example to check the monthly trend. The above figure is the chart of NIFTY on monthly charts. Here, the last candle of the current month is July 2021, and it is not yet completed and is under construction because we are in the middle of July. This candle still needs to be completed; it will be completed when the month ends. The second last white candle is of June, the third last of May, and so on. To analyse the monthly trend, we will compare our last white candle of June with its previous black candle of April. We are not considering July as the last candle because it is not yet complete. Here, it clearly shows that June is a white candle that has closed above its previous black candle, which was made in April. I have marked all the trends on all the candle charts from March 2020 for your understanding.

Let us start in March 2020. Here, the downturn continues from March to July. However, in August, the trend changed upward because the August candle was white, and it closed (11387.5) above the open price (11387.35) of its previous black candle, which was made in March 2020. So the August candle closed just 15 paise above the opening of the March 2020 black candle and reversed the trend of NIFTY in August 2020, and till July 2021, for almost ten months, the trend was continuously up.

Let us see what happened when we caught the right trend at the right moment. In August 2020, the NIFTY was at 11387; in nine months, it touched 15700, almost a 4000-point rally. So if someone has entered the market by making a buy position in NIFTY in august 2020, he must have gained almost 4000 points by catching the right trend.

PART C
APPLICABILITY OF UDTS©

CHAPTER 15

INTRADAY TRADING STRATEGIES ON CANDLES

In this chapter, I will discuss the intraday trading strategy on candle charts. This strategy is based on multi-frame time intervals to get the best results. We have included monthly, weekly, daily, intraday, and even 15-minute time intervals to get the best possible trend results. The strategy has 6 parameters, and once all the six parameters permit the trader to enter a trade, then only he should enter; otherwise, wait till the trader gets permission to enter a trade. All the intervals should show the trend in one direction. That means if the trend is bullish on one interval, it has to be bullish on all intervals. That is why we call the strategy Uni-Directional. Now, if all the intervals show a bullish trend, one must go for a bullish trade on that stock, and if all the intervals show a bearish trend, one must take a bear trade. So, let's check what the six bullish parameters are to take a bullish trade in a stock or index.

BULLISH PARAMETERS

If I am going to make an intraday trade in a particular stock I have selected based on news and data analysis, I will first check its monthly trend or trend on monthly interval charts.

First Parameter (EOD or End of the Day Parameter)

Monthly trend: If a monthly trend is up as per monthly candle charts, there is more probability of the stock going up in intraday too. This means news and data point the stock upward, and monthly charts also point the trend upward or show demand on the monthly charts. Now there are better chances that it will go up if I buy that stock on intraday. But still, I will get more confirmation from the weekly charts. Check an example of a monthly bullish trend on ICICI Bank (Fig. 1). Here is the chart of ICICI BANK on a monthly interval. That means each candle represents a complete month. You can go to https://investing.com or https://in.tradingview.com/ to study the charts. You can put candle charts at all the intervals you want. The image also shows where to click monthly charts on the https://investing.com website.

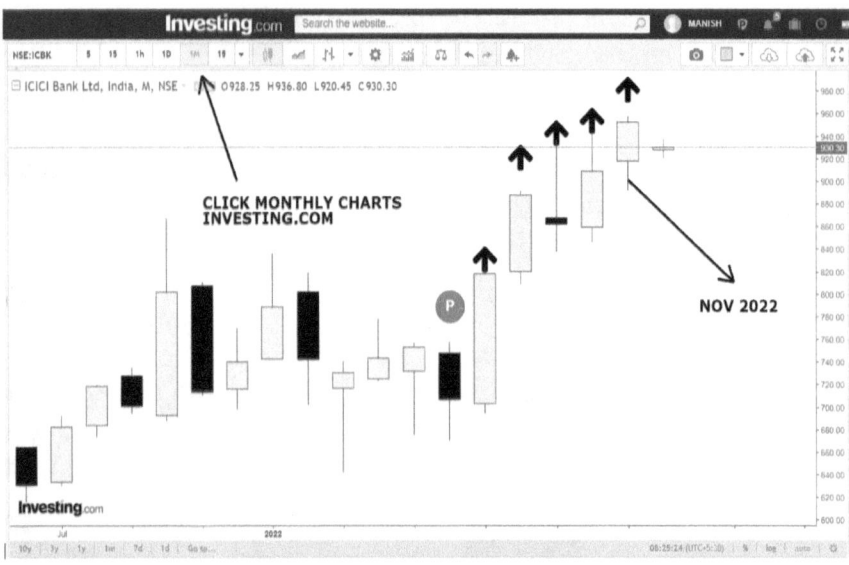

Monthly charts of ICICI Bank showing an upward trend (Fig. 1)

Second Parameter (EOD or End-Of-The-Day Parameter)

Weekly Trend: Once monthly charts show an upward trend, we will check the trend of the stock on weekly charts, and if weekly charts also show an upward trend, we will move to the 3rd parameter, i.e., the daily trend. Check Fig. 2 of ICICI Bank's weekly charts, which shows an upward trend. Here, each candle represents a full week, and as per trend analysis in the previous chapter, the trend of ICICI BANK on weekly charts is bullish as the last white candle is closing above the previous black candle. Here you can see a second last Black candle in Fig. 2, which can confuse you for a bear trend, but this black candle is not closed below the previous white candle. That's why the trend on this black candle is bullish.

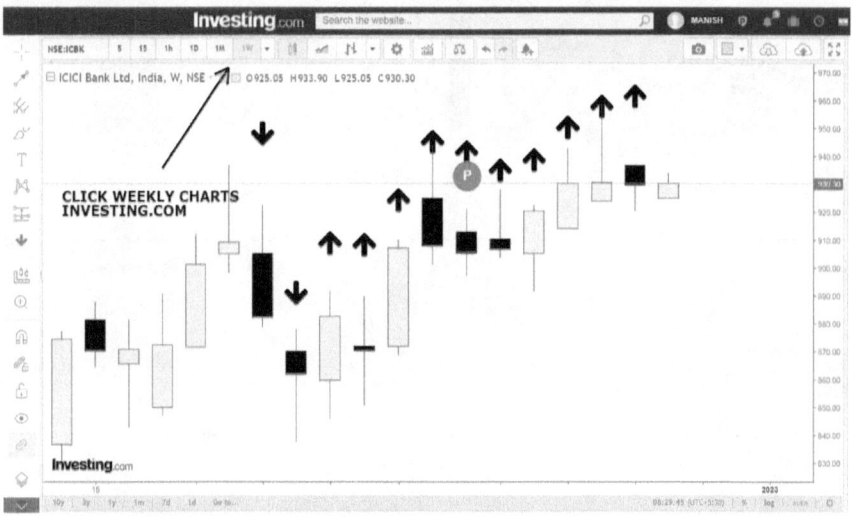

Weekly charts of ICICI Bank showing weekly trend up from the last ten weeks (Fig. 2)

Third Parameter (EOD or End-Of-The-Day Parameter)

Daily trend: After getting an upward trend from weekly charts, we will check the trend on daily charts. If daily charts also have an upward trend, we will read the 4th parameter. But if the daily parameter does not show an upward trend, we will not move to the next parameter to check the movement. Instead, we will leave this stock and look for another stock in which all the trends are going in the same direction. Check Fig. 3 to get a better understanding. Here the trend of ICICI BANK on daily charts is bullish.

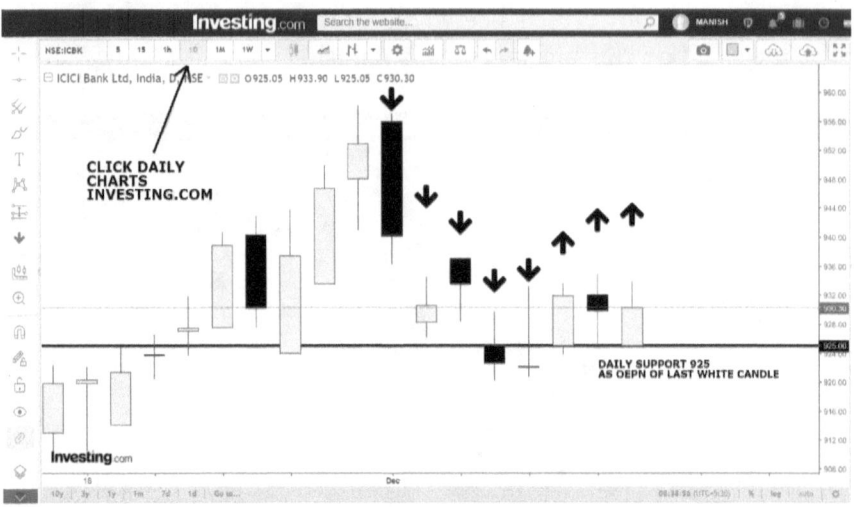

ICICI Bank's daily charts show an upward trend with
the daily support of 925 Fig. 3

Fourth Parameter (EOD or End-Of-The-Day Parameter)

The fourth parameter of the strategy says that the CMP (Current market price) should be above the daily Support-Now what is daily support? First, check the daily candle chart of ICICI BANK (Fig. 3), the stock on which we have already found an upward trend. On this chart, the opening price of the last white candle is your daily support, which is 925 (Fig. 3). Next, ensure the current-day candle you are trading is ignored. Does it seem complicated? Not at all. I will take many examples so that you can understand this point. Finally, if you have seen that CMP is above the daily support (Fig. 4), you will move forward to the 5th parameter, which is the biggest trend of the day.

15-minute candle charts ICICI Bank showing CMP 931, which is higher than daily support 925 (Fig. 4)

Fifth Parameter (Intraday Parameter)

The most significant trend of the day: The biggest trend is the most prominent trend between the two-time points. If CMP is above daily support and stock is in an upward trend on monthly, weekly, and daily charts, you also have to check demand on intraday charts. The first four parameters are based on an EOD (End-Of-The-Day), but the fifth parameter is an intraday parameter. So you have to check this on a 15-minute intraday chart. At the time of the trade, you have to check the most significant trend from 9:15 a.m. to 10:15 a.m. if you are taking the trade at 10:15 a.m. For example, if you are taking the trade at 10 a.m., you have to check the complete trend from 9:15 a.m. to 10 a.m. And if you are taking the entry at 12 p.m., then, in that case, you have to check the most significant trend from 9:15 a.m. to 12 p.m. If this trend is also up, we will move to the 6th parameter further. Fig. 5 shows the intraday biggest trend of ICICI BANK on 15min candle charts from 9 a.m. to 10 a.m. is bullish.

Fig. 5: Showing biggest trend from 9:15 a.m. to 10 a.m. (pointing a to b) 45-minute trend (biggest trend till 10 a.m.) is upwards on ICICI Bank.

Sixth Parameter

15-Minute Trend: If all the above parameters point the stock upward, then we will check the last parameter, which is a trend on 15-minute candle charts. If on 15-minute candles, the trend is also showing upward, then that is called Uni-Directional Price Movement on all intervals. That is the time when you can enter a trade with full confidence on the buying side.

Fig. 6 shows a 15-minute upward trend on ICICI Bank

When all the forces—monthly, weekly, daily, and intraday—are in the same direction, that will be the direction of that stock for the next few Minutes or Hours. And, as intraday traders, we all know we are opportunistic people. Once we see all the forces in an upward direction, there is a very high chance that the stock will go up in price, or if a trader buys the stock at that time, we can have the highest winning probability. The first four parameters are on an EOD basis; these are the parameters you can see on charts a day before the trading day. If I want to trade tomorrow, I can prepare a list of stocks for buying or selling a day before as my homework.

INTRADAY TRADING STRATEGIES	
1 – Monthly Trend Upward/Downward	EOD
2 – Weekly Trend Upward/Downward	
3 – Daily Trend Upward/Downward	
4 – (CMP) Current Market Price should be Above/Below Daily Support/Resistance	
5 – Biggest Trend of the Day should be Bullish/Bearish	
6 – 15-minute Trend should be Bullish/Bearish	

Six parameters of intraday trading strategy:

Finally, we have understood the bullish parameters of the UDTS© intraday strategy.

If all six parameters are bullish, it means a high demand in stock indicates a high chance of prices going up in the short term.

Bearish Parameters

Let's talk about bearish parameters. If all the parameters show a downward trend, the stock has a high supply, and the chances of going down in price are much higher. Let's understand if a stock has the following:

- The monthly trend is down
- Weekly trend down
- Daily trend down

- CMP is below daily resistance-
- The biggest intraday trend is down
- The 15-minute trend is down

Here we have seen that all the parameters show the downward direction of a stock and are Uni-Directional on the downside. That means the stock has a higher chance of going down in price, and traders should use the first sell-then-buy strategy.

It means you have to sell the stock at a price, and when it goes down, you will buy it for a lesser price and book profits. So many people need clarification about how they can sell a stock when I am not holding it. But in intraday trading, we are not going to deliver the stock, and that's why we have to cover the stock before 3 p.m.; that's why we can sell the stock between 9:15 a.m. and 3 p.m., but the condition is that we have to cover it compulsorily before 3 p.m. If you don't cover the stock, the broker will, by default, cover the stock on your behalf if you have told him about the intraday trade. Suppose the broker also does not cover the stock on your behalf. In that case, you will face an action penalty from the relevant exchange on which you are trading. Thus, it is essential that if you sell a trade intraday, you never take a chance to leave without squaring up. This way, intraday traders can make money in bearish trends too.

Finally, if all six parameters are bearish, it means there is a high supply of stock, and it has a high chance of going down in price in the short term.

Now let's understand the strategy parameters by an example.

We will use UDTS© Screeners to find bullish or bearish stocks. It has two parts, i.e., UDTS© Monitor and UDTS© Intraday Screener.

https://www.ifmcinstitute.com/UDTS-intraday-screener/

Readers can also check our online recorded course at https://www.ifmcinstitute.com/online-stock-market-courses/uni-directional-trading-strategies/ for a detailed understanding.

UDTS© Monitor is a free version that helps find bullish stocks on EOD charts that are on monthly, weekly, and daily intervals. We save a lot of time finding bullish and bearish stocks from over 3000 stocks on NSE and BSE.

UDTS© Intraday Screener is a paid version by IFMC to find bullish and bearish stocks on EOD and Intraday charts. It helps save traders time by allowing them to select bullish or bearish stocks according to UDTS© principles while intraday trading.

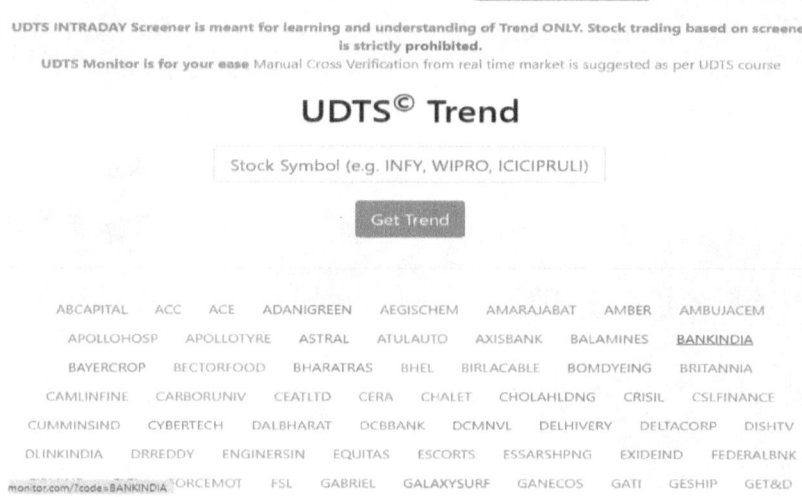

Fig. 2 UDTS© Monitor screenshot

Here is the screenshot of the UDTS© Monitor in Fig. 2. It shows some stocks in the green and some in red. Green stocks are bullish on monthly, weekly, and daily parameters, and red stocks are bearish on monthly, weekly, and daily charts. This is a learning tool for students to fetch stocks with demand or supply quickly. You must check all the parameters manually also to make a final view. Let's click on AB CAPITAL, the first green stock on the screen.

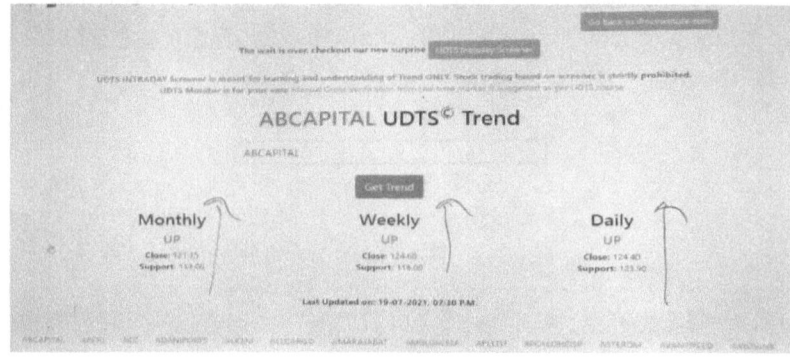

Fig.3 AB CAPITAL

As in Fig. 3, all three parameters of AB CAPITAL are bullish. The screener also shows the support levels on all three intervals, i.e., monthly, weekly and daily. If we want to take an intraday trade, our first three parameters are through. Now you only have to check the three intraday parameters on the trading day, which you can check from https://investing.com, or you can further take help from UDTS© Intraday Screener (paid version) for intraday parameters at a quick glance.

Let's take some examples:

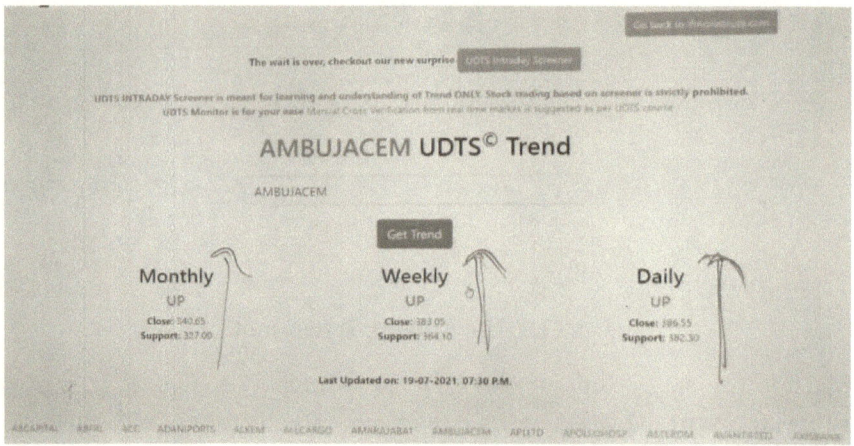

Let's take the example of Ambuja Cement. All three EOD parameters are upwards. (Fig. 4)

Now I am going to make a trade-in Ambuja Cement as an example. Here Fig. 4 shows Ambuja cement is up on all three parameters. Now I am going to check this manually on https://investing.com. I will use this site to show you charts. It's absolutely free.

Chapter 15: Intraday Trading Strategies On Candles | 87

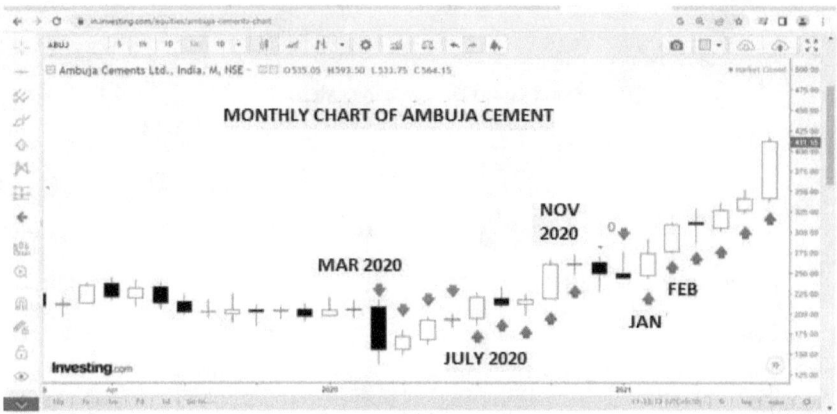

Fig. 5 Ambuja Cement

I will make a demo trade at 10 a.m. today (20 July 2021) if all six parameters match. This is the monthly chart of Ambuja Cement (Fig. 5).

First, I will manually check all six chart parameters, then decide or create a view to buy or sell this stock. I have marked the trend from March 2020 onwards to give you more understanding. In March, April, May, and June, Ambuja was on a downtrend, but from July, it reversed and became bullish till November 2020. Then in December and January, it was again in a downtrend, and from Feb 2021 to June 2021, it was bullish.

So, now, Ambuja is in an upward trend on the monthly charts. After monthly parameters, we move forward and go to the next parameter, which is the weekly trend.

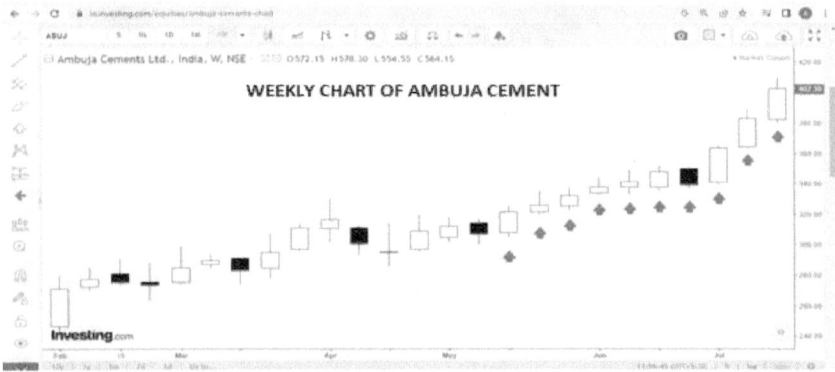

Fig.6

So, here you can see the weekly trend (Fig. 6), which is also upward. So, now our two trends are in the same direction, and that is upward.

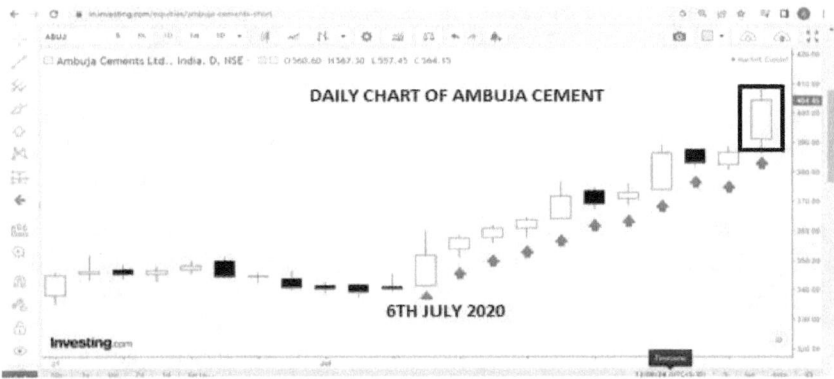

Fig. 7

Now let's go to the third parameter, which is a daily trend. This is our daily chart reference Fig. 7. The last candle on Fig. 7 shows 20 July as the trading day. This candle is to be ignored as it is still in the making process as it is a daily trend candle, and the day is not finished yet as we are going to make the trade at 10 a.m. on 20 July. We have to consider the 2nd last candle of 19 July. Here I have marked the trend from 6 July 2021 to 19 July 2021. You see, from 6 July, not even a single time has the trend gone down. The daily trend is continuously up from 6 July till 19 July. Finally, we have seen that its daily trend is also upward. Now let's move to the next parameter.

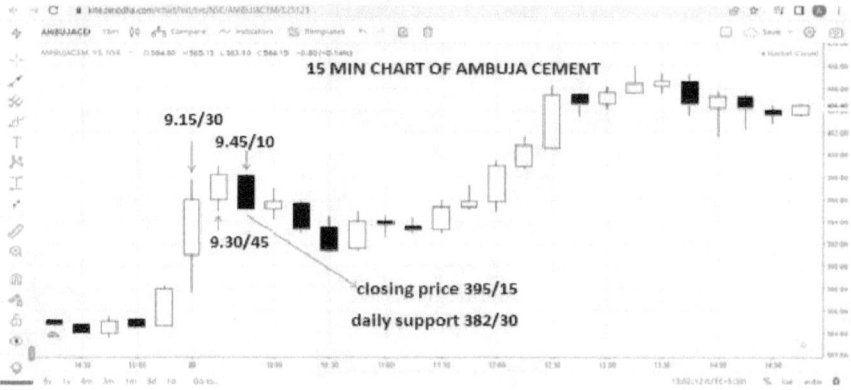

Fig. 8

Now, in Fig. 8 above, I have shown a 15-minute candle chart starting from 9:15 a.m. as the first 15-minute candle of the day. By 10 a.m., the price of Ambuja cement was ₹395.15, which is above its daily support of ₹382.3 (explained in Fig. 9).

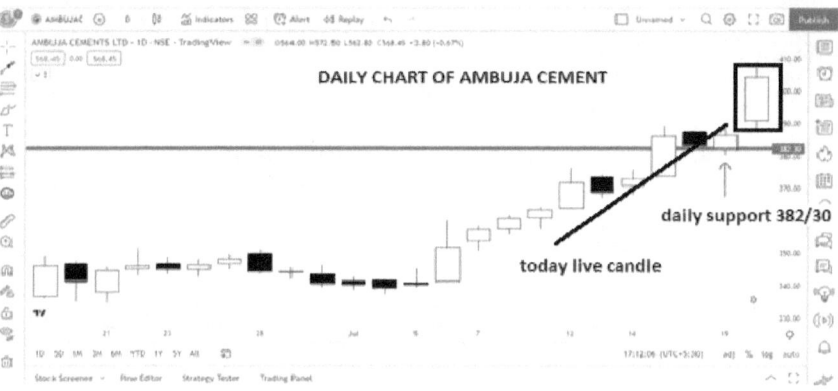

Fig. 9 Daily support at ₹382.3

Now by 10 a.m., four parameters are matched. Let's quickly move on to the 5th parameter. The biggest trend is the trend that started from where the day started and till the time we are going to take a position.

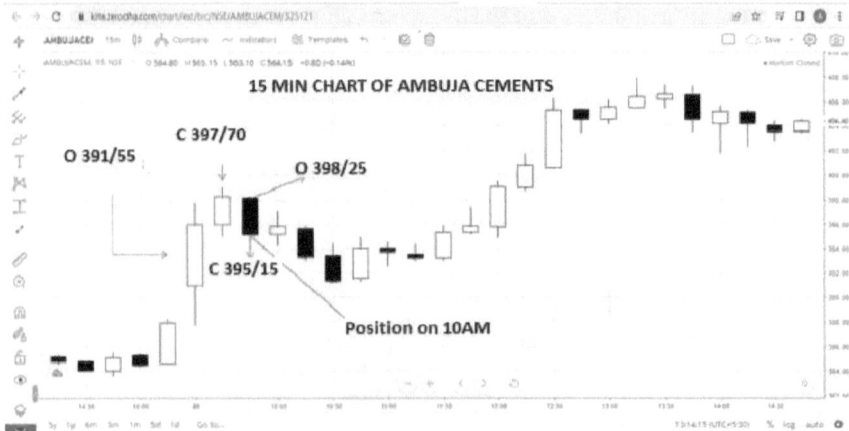

Fig.10 Biggest trend

Let's say we are taking a position at 10 a.m. Until 10 a.m., the biggest trend here starts at 9:15 a.m. and finishes at 10 a.m., so I have to see that trend during this time period. There are three candles, and out of these three candles, we have to identify whether the biggest trend is bullish or bearish. The open price of the first white candle of the day was ₹391.55, and this bull trend ended at the close of the 2nd candle at ₹397.7, meaning the bull trend was almost ₹6.15 (i.e., 397.7-391.55) points, and on the 3rd black candle, the bear trend was ₹3.1 (i.e., 398.25-397.7) points.

So, until 10 a.m., the biggest trend was bullish with 6.15 points.

Now for the last and final parameter. If this parameter also gives me a bullish sign, then there will be no technical reason to say that the stock will not rise in price.

Fig. 11 15-minute chart Ambuja Cement

At 10 a.m., the 3rd candle is black and closed below the previous white candle. That means the 15-minute trend is downward at 10 a.m.

Now all five parameters have matched, but the 6th parameter of the 15-minute trend does not match. In this case, we have to wait to buy the stock. And you may have noticed that from the 3rd candle, the price started sliding down till it reached ₹391.4 on the 6th black candle of the day. This is the power of each and every parameter. My last 15-minute parameter stopped me from entering the trade, which is called a mechanism, as the parameters of the strategy work like a machine with no emotional inputs.

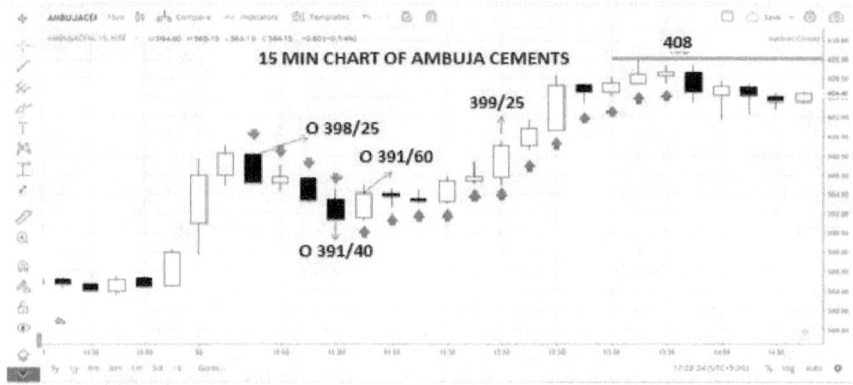

Fig. 12

As we advance, after the 12th white candle of the day, when the price was ₹399.25 (reference Fig. 12), all the parameters matched again. Check Fig. 13; here, the biggest trend was again up, and the 15-minute trend was also up. At this time, the price of Ambuja was ₹399.25. At that point, when all the parameters match, we can buy the stock, or you can say that this is the perfect or **unchallenged entry point** that we got at 12 p.m., where the stop-loss will be the opening of the biggest trend, which is ₹391.6.

Fig. 13

Now just see the charts after entering the trade just after five candles of 15-minute Ambuja touched the levels of 408 (refer to Fig. 13). That means after entering the trade, you reached the exit point in just one hour with almost 2% gains. This is why a trader should patiently wait for the right time like a lion, and once he gets the opportunity to enter, he should grab it with full confidence.

Important Guiding points to execute UDTS STRATEGY

STOP-LOSS AS PER UDTS© STRATEGY

Now, after understanding the six parameters of the UDTS© intraday strategy, we got to know what to buy and when to buy. Now the next question arises: When to sell or when to exit a trade?

According to UDTS© intraday strategy, stop-loss would be the open price of the biggest trend.

This means if I buy a stock at ₹100 at 10 a.m. on a particular day. At that time, the open price of the biggest trend was ₹98. Then, if any 15-minute black candle closes below ₹98, I will have to exit the trade, or I will cut my stop-loss. Here, the most important thing is that you should wait for the black candle to complete. If a black candle is closed below ₹98, it implies the price has sustained for at least some time below the support level of ₹98.

You don't have to cut your positions on the shadows of the candle. Shadows are made with temporary price movements, which are not trustworthy.

Let's take some examples:

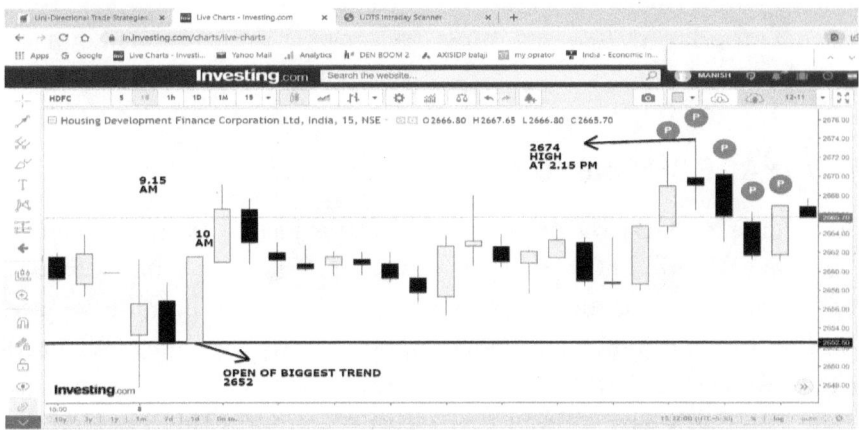

HDFC 15-minute charts – opening of biggest trends at 9:15 a.m.

In the above chart, at 10 a.m., the biggest trend was bullish, and the 15-minute trend at 10 a.m. was also bullish. A trader can take a buy position at 10 a.m. with a stop-loss in mind of 2652, as 2652 is the opening price from where the biggest trend started. Till 2:15 p.m., you can see that no black candle had breached 2652. Though HDFC came near 2652 around 12 p.m., it could not breach 2652, and by 2:15 p.m., it made a high of 2674.

WHAT SHOULD BE THE TARGETS AS PER UDTS© PRINCIPLES?

As per UDTS© principles, the 1st target should be 1%, and the 2nd target should be 2%. This means if you enter a trade by buying 500 shares at ₹100 each, you will put 50% of your position, which is 250 shares, to sell at ₹101, and for the rest of the 50%, you will sell at ₹102.

Intraday trading is a game of quickness and mental alertness. As soon as you buy a stock, you have to place your 1st and 2nd target at the same time when you initiate the trade. This means you will put three orders at the same time, one for buying the stock and two orders to place the 1st and 2nd targets. This will reduce your mental pressure as, sometimes, stocks are so volatile that they can achieve the targets in the next 5 to 15 minutes. If your order is placed timely, you will not lose the opportunity to sell and book your profits.

As an intraday trader, you must try to exit the trade as soon as possible.

NO TRADE BEFORE 10 A.M.

According to UDTS© principles, no trade has to be taken before 10 a.m. We all know markets open at 9:15 a.m., but UDTS© advocates not to trade before 10 a.m. in any case because we are trading on charts, not on emotions, nor are we gambling. We need charts to see the chart pattern, and on the basis of charts, we make a view, and that's why we wait for at least 45 minutes after opening the market so that we can have at least three 15-minute candles to study the trend.

So, my dear friends, be patient, as we know that patience pays everywhere, and the stock market is no exception. Many people start buying and selling as soon as the market opens on the basis of the previous day's candle charts. That's not right, as every day is new for the stock market, and every day has a different trend. So it's better to trade after 10 a.m. when the market settles.

UNCHALLENGED POINTS OF ENTRY AND EXIT

As per UDTS©, the unchallenged point of entry is where all six parameters of an intraday trading strategy meet. At this point in time, we find maximum demand for all the intervals—monthly, weekly, daily, and intraday. Whereas the exit point is where all the sell parameters of the UDTS© strategy meet. At that point, there is maximum supply at all intervals. If you have also studied technical analysis and put all the technical tools at these points, you will find that 90% of the technical tools will also suggest the same trend as UDTS©.

THE BIGGEST TREND OF THE DAY

Let's understand the biggest trend of the day. At whatever time I am going to make the trade at that time, I have to check the biggest trend from the beginning of the day, which is 9:15 a.m. In the NIFTY chart below, from 9:15 a.m. until 10 a.m., the biggest trend was bullish, and if I check the biggest trend at 11 a.m., the biggest trend changed to bearish.

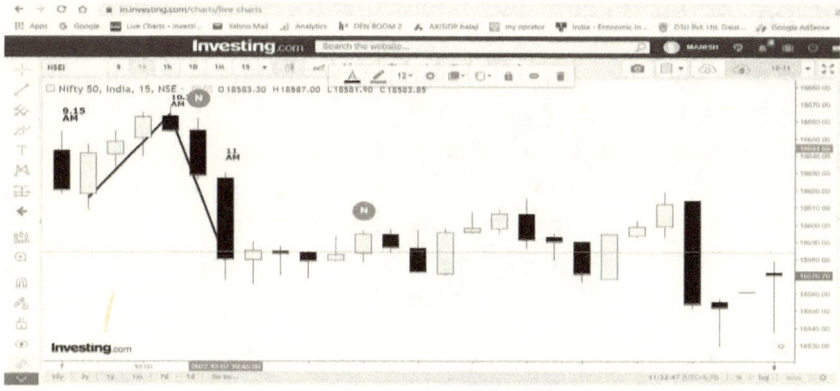

NIFTY 15-minute chart showing the biggest intraday trend

So at whatever time you are entering the trade, at that time, you have to check the biggest trend, followed by the 15-minute trend.

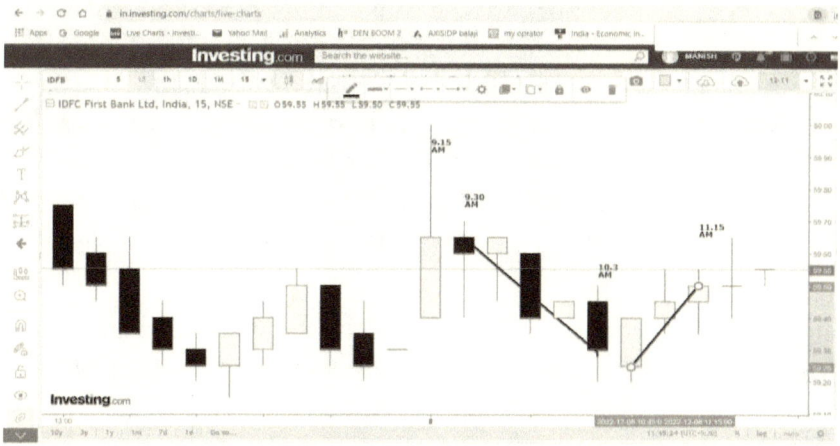

IDFC First 15-minute charts

Let's take one more example of IDFC First Bank on the above 15-minute candle charts. Here, if I want to take a trade and check for the biggest trend at 11:15 a.m., it's clear from the size of the trend line that the biggest trend until 11:15 a.m. is bearish because the downward trend from 9:30 a.m. to 10:30 a.m. is bigger than the upward trend from 10:45 a.m. to 11.15 a.m.

DEFINITION OF SUPPORT AND RESISTANCE AS PER UDTS© PRINCIPLES

Understanding support and resistance is very important for traders. Support and resistance points are not technically the points of stop-loss. Normally, traders think if support or resistance is breached, they have to exit their positions and book losses as their stop-losses are hit. But as they exit the positions, the stock makes a U-turn and reaches new highs or lows. This can be very frustrating for young traders. Let's understand the concept thoroughly.

Support and resistance are imaginary lines drawn on charts that show at that point or price, and the stock gathers huge demand or supply according to the trading intervals. Support price basically indicates to the trader that near to that price (not exact) stock gets demand from the market. In the same way, resistance prices also indicate that near the resistance, the stock gets supplied in the market. These points are referral points of demand and supply, not exact points. Whenever a stock comes near support, maybe some points down or some points up, it can get demand from the market. Similarly, if a stock goes near the resistance point, maybe some points above or below, it can get supplied. There will be different support and resistance prices for different intervals. Support on monthly charts shows the price where the stock has demand on broader intervals of 30 to 40 days, and resistance on monthly charts shows supply on monthly intervals of 30 to 40 days.

Support and resistance on the weekly chart show demand and supply in stock at a 7 to 10-day interval. In the same way, it works on daily and intraday charts also.

Chapter 15: Intraday Trading Strategies On Candles | 97

Let's understand this through the charts:

NIFTY Monthly Chart support at 18130, where the current price is 18600

In the above monthly chart of NIFTY, monthly support is at 18130, and the current market price is 18600. Here, the support of 18130 implies that whenever NIFTY comes between the range of 18000 and 18200, it is in the major support range, or it can see demand in this area at any time. Here, 18130 also indicates that if the price of NIFTY sustains below 18130, we can say the support range is broken, and after that, NIFTY can go further down.

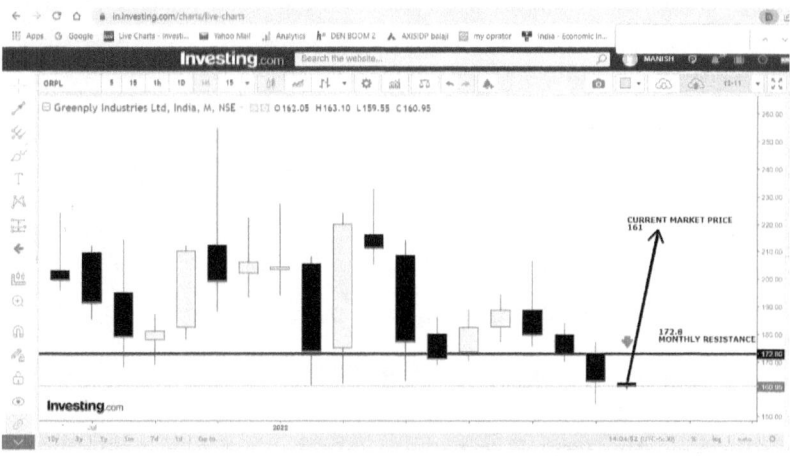

Monthly Chart of Greenply – monthly resistance at 172.8 and CMP is 161

In the above image, you can see the monthly resistance of Greenply is 172.8 and CMP is 161, which means if the price of Greenply rises and it sustains above the resistance, then only we can say resistance is breached, but if it breaches 172.8 but cannot sustain above 172.8, the price resistance, in that case, is not breached, and if a trader has a sell position in Greenply he should wait.

Finally, a trader has to wait for some time to check whether the support or resistance is breached with sustenance.

WHAT IS THE MEANING OF SUSTENANCE?

Sustenance means to hold over or below any price for some time. It is the most common factor when a trader says his stop-loss is always a hit, and once the stop-loss hits, the stock immediately takes a U-turn and touches a new high. 90% of the traders face this problem, and the only reason is that they cut their stop-losses in the shadow of the candle. This means the price could not hold below the support or above the resistance. Price has to sustain after breaching the stop-loss levels. If not, then go with the trade.

Traders put the stop-losses on the support or resistance points, and when the stock reaches near those points and makes volatile movements, the stop-loss gets hit due to spikes in price, but the stock cannot hold that level as it gets huge demand if it is near the support level or it gets huge supply when it is near the resistance level.

So as per UDTS© principles, one has to give sustenance time below or above the support or resistance levels according to the interval of support or resistance.

Sustenance time for monthly support or resistance

If the price breaches monthly support or resistance, then you know the month has 24 trading days, so at least $1/3^{rd}$ of the time (at least 8 to 9 days), the price has to sustain above or below the monthly support or resistance levels.

Sustenance time for weekly support or resistance

In the case of weekly levels, if at least two daily candles close below support or two daily candles close above resistance, we can say the price has sustained below or above support or resistance levels.

Sustenance time for daily support or resistance

In the case of daily levels, at least one hourly candle should close above the resistance or one hourly candle close below the support. In this case, we can say the stop-loss is breached as the price has sustained below support or above resistance.

Let me take one more example of intraday trading:

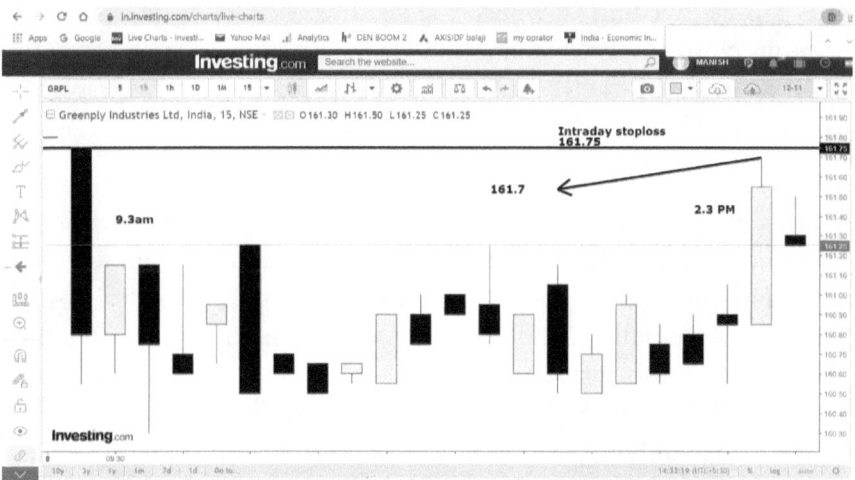

Greenply 15-minute charts intraday resistance at 161.75

Here is a 15-minute chart of Greenply, which has an intraday resistance at 161.75, marked on the 9:15 a.m. candle. By 2:30 p.m., it rose and tried to touch 161.75 but faced resistance, and it again came down. If we are making an intraday trade and we have a sell position on Greenply, then we should not cut the position immediately if it breaches 161.75; rather, we should wait for a 15-minute white candle to close above 161.75 levels. If any white 15-minute candle closes above the intraday resistance of 161.75, we must cut our stop-loss. That's why, according to UDTS©, we do not place stop-loss orders in advance in intraday trading because stop-losses can be cut by shadows as well, and UDTS© does not give any importance to shadows. Only if a white candle is made above resistance or a black candle is made below intraday support, only then we can square up our trade.

I hope you have a clear understanding of the concepts of support and resistance.

GAP-UP OR GAP-DOWN OPENING

Now a very important question arises: What to do if a stock is bullish on all parameters of the UDTS©, but has made a Gap-up opening? The gap-up opening is when a stock opens much higher than its previous close because of some sudden news inflow. In such cases, the CMP (Current Market Price) and the open price of the biggest trend have a huge difference in price.

For example, a stock has a gap opening at 105, almost 5% higher than its previous closing. So many times, when we make the trade at 10 a.m., there may be more than a 5% to 6% difference between the CMP and our support price. This is a very tricky situation because all parameters are bullish, and if we buy a trade that retraces and closes below our support price, we have to incur more than a 7% to 8% loss in a single trade. So in such a situation, we should not buy 100% quantity to avoid big risks.

We can enter a trade with only 50% quantity, and if the price comes near to our support price intraday, we can add a further 50% of our quantity. And if it does not come down and rises more, then we should be happy with 50% profits only. To summarise, avoid the trades which have more than 2% stop-loss intraday.

TRADING CONCEPTS

Now that we understand the Intraday Trading Strategy, let's understand some of the basic rules and styles of an intraday trader. Let me clear this up with some good examples.

In my opinion, a trader should act like a lion. His psych should be that of a lion if he wants to catch the perfect trade. Just like a lion catches its prey in a jungle, the trader must also possess the following virtues to be successful:

- Focus
- Patience
- Emotionless
- Confident
- Escape route

The first thing that a lion does is focus on its prey. It single-mindedly selects one prey from far away. A trader should similarly select particular stocks before a trading day as homework in which he wants to take a bullish or bearish position.

Secondly, have patience. Like a lion moving patiently toward its target, a trader should wait patiently for the right moment. Wait for the stock to come into your range and grab it without emotional attachment like a lion who mercilessly pounces on its prey.

Be confident in yourself and your strategy, as a flinch can make your trade go awry.

Have an escape plan if you cannot catch your prey? If you experience a string of losses in the stock market, you must have an exit strategy or an "escape route". And that is stop-loss. This will help you to minimise your losses and protect your investment portfolio.

Let's now understand some more concepts:

1. Trade Like a Thief

A trader must act and think like a thief. Just as a thief takes a complete note of the house, people, and timetable, keeps track of movement, and finally decides a time to get in the place. Similarly, a trader must also track all stock market activities and choose the right time to enter.

Also, a thief never waits in the house; he just picks up the things and makes a quick exit. Similarly, a trader must also make quick exits as soon as the targets are hit and should collect all his returns. He must also exit the trades if a stop-loss gets hit, as hitting a stop-loss is like buying an alarm.

A thief also has an alternate plan to move out if caught in some unfavourable circumstances. Thus, a trader must plan, execute, and make a quick exit and have alternate plans of exit in his mind because the trader has a limited time in which he has to find an opportunity, book profits, and exit.

2. Always Stay Behind Bull or Bear Whoever is more powerful

A trader, as I say, is an opportunist, and the common man doesn't have enough capital to change the direction of the market, so the better way is to identify the strengths and be with them or behind them. If bulls are powerful, then he should be with the bulls, and if bears are powerful, then he should be with the bears. This is what I call being in trend, or when I say trader should be in trend.

Trader Should Stay Behind Who Ever Is More Powerful

If the Bear is powerful, then the trader should stay behind the Bears and wait for the opportunities to Sell first and then buy.

Trader Should Stay Behind Who Ever Is More Powerful

If the Bull is powerful, the traders should stay behind the Bulls and wait for the opportunities to buy first and then sell.

CHAPTER 16

SHORT-TERM POSITIONAL TRADING STRATEGY ON CANDLES

We have already discussed finding the unchallenged entry and exit points. If we find a point where we get the maximum demand at all intervals, we try to create a buy or bullish position. Vice versa, if we get to a point with maximum supply, we will try to sell and take a bearish position.

You have already understood the concept of finding these points from the intraday trading strategy in the previous chapter. Now, there is little change in the short-term positional trading strategy on candles. All six parameters are the same as in intraday trading strategy, but the only difference is stop-loss and target. This means the entry point is the same as the intraday trading strategy; only the exit point is different.

In short-term positional trading, the stop-loss will be:

If any hourly candle closes above or below the daily resistance or support, the stop-loss is breached.

For example: If you buy a stock at ₹100 when all six intraday trading parameters are met and carry forward your position to the next day with a stop-loss of ₹95 as daily support. In that case, if any black hourly candle is closed below ₹95, you will have to exit the trade, or you can say that your stop-loss is breached.

And if you sell a stock at ₹100 when all intraday trading parameters are met and carry forward your position to the next day with a stop-loss of ₹105 as daily resistance, and if any white hourly candle closes above the daily resistance of ₹105, then you have to exit the trade, or your stop-loss is hit.

Now we'll talk about the target. In intraday, our targets were 1% to 2%, and here, the targets will be at least 3% to 5% in short-term positional.

Live Market Examples

Short-term positional trade on Ambuja cement on 20 July 2021

We are going to discuss Ambuja Cement (Fig. 1).

Fig. 1 (15-minute chart of Ambuja cement) *Dated 20/07/2021*

On 20 July 2021, we got an entry point around 12 p.m. at ₹399, and if we wanted to enter a buy-side short-term positional trade in Ambuja Cement, which closed at ₹401 on 20 July, then our stop-loss would've been ₹382.5 (which is daily support).

Fig. 2

Above is Ambuja Cement's daily candle chart (refer to Fig. 2), showing daily support at ₹382.3. The last candle is of 20 July, and the second last candle is of 19 July, which has an opening price of ₹382.3.

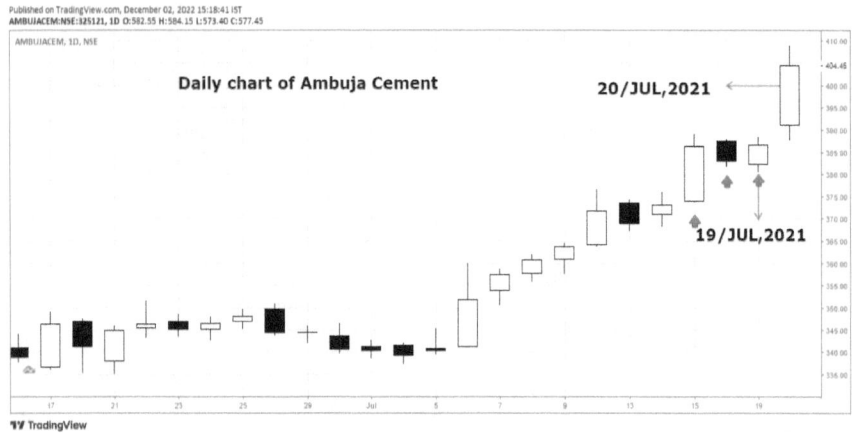

Fig. 3 Ambuja Cement daily candle chart

Fig. 4 Ambuja Cement closing at 387.95 on 19 July

Let's go with one more example (reference Fig. 4). If, on 19 July, we would have entered Ambuja Cement at the closing price at 3 p.m. at ₹387.95 (check Fig. 4) when all the entry parameters were met.

In that case, we can carry the trade to the next day with the stop-loss of ₹382.3 (the daily support 19 July 2021 take reference Fig. 3).

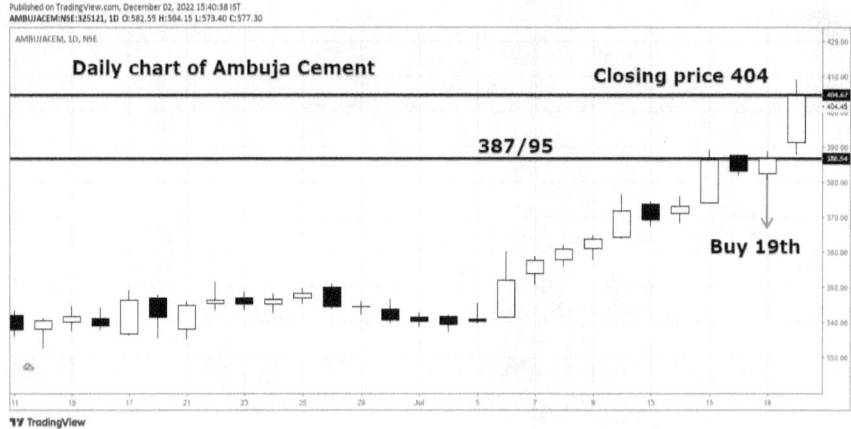

Fig. 5 Ambuja Cement closed 404 on 20 July, touching a high of 408

On the next day, Ambuja touched a high of ₹408 on 20 July 2021, giving away almost 4% to 5% returns (reference Fig. 5).

I hope you all have understood the concept of short-term positional trading. I have tried to give you maximum examples so you can understand the concepts well.

Next, let's move on to the medium-term positional strategy.

CHAPTER 17
MEDIUM-TERM POSITIONAL TRADING STRATEGY ON CANDLES

In previous chapters, we learned intraday and short positional trading strategies, and in this chapter, we will understand the medium-term positional trading strategy on candles.

The medium-term positional trading strategy has no significant changes to the intraday trading strategy. All six parameters are the same as in intraday trading, but the only difference is stop-loss and target. This means the entry point is the same as the intraday trading strategy; only the exit points differ.

In medium-term positional trading, the stop-loss will be:

If any daily candle closes above or below the weekly resistance or support, the stop-loss is breached.

For example:

If you bought a stock at ₹100 and carried forward your position for the next 4 to 5 days with a weekly stop-loss of ₹90, and if any daily black candle is closed below ₹90, exit the trade, or your stop-loss will be breached.

If you sell a stock at ₹100 and carry forward your position to the next 4-5 days with a weekly stop-loss of ₹110. If any white daily candle closes above the weekly resistance of ₹110, you have to exit the trade, or your stop-loss is hit.

Now I'll discuss the target. During intraday, our targets were 1% to 2%. Here the targets will be at least 5% to 10% in medium-term positional trading.

CHAPTER 18
LONG-TERM POSITIONAL TRADING STRATEGY ON CANDLES

In this chapter, we will understand the long-term positional trading strategy. The long-term positional trading strategy has no significant changes to the intraday trading strategy. All six parameters are the same as in intraday trading, but the only difference is stop-loss and target.

This means the entry point is the same as the intraday trading strategy; only the exit points differ.

In long-term positional trading, the stop-loss will be:

If any weekly candle closes above or below the monthly resistance or support, the stop-loss is breached.

For example:

If you bought a stock at ₹100 and carried forward your position for the next 25 to 45 days with a monthly stop-loss of ₹85, and if any weekly black candle is closed below the monthly support of ₹85, you will have to exit the trade, or you can say that your stop-loss is breached.

If you sell a stock at ₹100 and carry forward your position to the next 25 to 45 days with a monthly stop-loss of ₹115, and if any weekly white candle closes above the monthly resistance at ₹115, you have to exit the trade, or your stop-loss is hit.

Now we talk about the target. Intraday, our targets were 1% to 2%. Here the targets will be at least 12% to 20% in long-term positional trading.

CHAPTER 19

TRADE MODEL-TO ACHIEVE REGULAR INCOME FROM INTRADAY TRADING

Besides the strategy, what are the other factors to be considered to raise my winning probabilities?

>>— chakravyuh →

The stock market is like the Chakravyuh of **the Mahabharata.** Anyone can enter, but only a few know how to exit as Arjun does. The right strategy helps you come out of this Chakravyuh. To earn regularly from the stock market, you must understand that you can't win 100% of the trades, but yes, you can succeed in 7-8 trades out of 10. If you can correctly forecast the price movement of 7-8 trades out of 10, your accuracy will be 75% to 80%. You have to keep increasing this probability to 80-90% with your practice and experience.

Chapter 19 : Trade Model-To Achieve Regular Income from Intraday Trading

The UDTS© trade model works on multiple time frames and includes various factors like news analysis, NIFTY trend, sectoral analysis, and basket trading, along with individual stock trends at all intervals. It helps achieve a high success rate. With 80-85% accuracy, you can achieve your target of a regular income from the stock market through intraday trading.

According to the UDTS© trade model, you can raise your winning probabilities through different parameters as below:

PARAMETERS	WEIGHTAGE OF PARAMETER
By Right News analysis	5%
NIFTY Trend	5%
Sectoral Analysis	5%
Trade Basket	5%
Individual Stock Trend	
Monthly Parameter	5%
Weekly Trend	10%
Daily Trend	15%
Intraday Trend	20%
Practice And Experience	15%
Total	85 % Approx.

The above table is for educational purposes only, to explain how each and every parameter helps in raising the winning probability of a trader. This table is for reference and explanation purposes only. We do not recommend live market trades based on the above table. Please check the table authenticity with paper trades only.

Let's check this with a perfect Trade Model made by IFMC®.

The trade model is important when it comes to the Application of a Strategy. Now is the time to apply it properly to get the desired result.

Along with a set of rules and disciplines, we have covered different parameters and regulations during live trading in the previous section.

IFMC® Trade Model	
News + Data Analysis	VIEW
UDTS© (Uni-Directional Trade Strategy)	VIEW

STEP 1 – MAKING VIEW BY NEWS AND DATA

I have already told you about news and data analysis. So the first thing you need to do in the morning is to check the overall news and data, i.e., macro data. I'm not talking about micro because I know all my students do not have an economics background. But everyone knows something about macro. At least you people are reading the newspaper daily, which is sufficient. So whatever the news is, it is adequate to understand the market's overall movement and make a view bullish or bearish. On the other hand, suppose we get positive data on GDP and comprehensive news for a particular day is positive. In that case, we will move to the next step with a bullish approach.

STEP 2 - TECHNICAL VIEW ON NIFTY

In the second step, make a technical view of NIFTY or Sensex according to the UDTS© strategy. As we all know, the market is brilliant and discounts every news item and data that is already published.

You will find one of the six combinations of trends mentioned below in NIFTY as per UDTS (three) EOD Parameters.

- Case 1 - Monthly Up, Weekly Up, Daily Up
- Case 2 - Monthly Up, Weekly Up, Daily Down
- Case 3 - Monthly Up, Weekly Down, Daily Down
- Case 4 - Monthly Down, Weekly Down, Daily Down
- Case 5 - Monthly Down, Weekly Down, Daily Up
- Case 6 - Monthly Down, Weekly Up, Daily Up

This trend analysis of NIFTY will give me a clear picture of the market. It will help me in the next step of making the basket.

STEP 3 - MAKING A BASKET

As I have already told you, a trader should trade with the highest probability of winning as he is not a gambler. In this step, we will create a basket where I will keep at least four stocks for intraday trading. Because if I trade in a single stock with my entire trading amount, the stock might not perform or may hit my stop-loss, giving me losses. But if I make a basket of four trades with the same trading amount, I will improve my winning probabilities.

Now the question is: How to make the basket?

Here Step 2 will help us in making baskets. According to step number 2, we will choose how many bullish and bearish stocks we have to keep in the basket.

- Case 1 - 3 Buy and 1 Sell
- Case 2 - 2 Buy and 2 Sell
- Case 3 - 2 Buy and 2 Sell
- Case 4 - 3 Sell and 1 Buy
- Case 5 - 2 Sell and 2 Buy
- Case 6 - 2 Sell and 2 Buy

Suppose the news is positive and NIFTY is bullish on monthly, weekly, and daily intervals. In that case, we will select Case 1 and make a basket with three bullish and one bearish stock.

Now you can ask: If news and NIFTY trends both show highly positive signs, why are we still taking one bearish trade in our basket?

In previous chapters, I told you that while trading, you should always be hedged, and this one bear trade is a hedge trade that will help you in adverse circumstances. For example, if any bad news comes in intraday and the market takes a sharp U-turn, in that case, it may happen that all the stop-losses of your bullish trades hit. In that case, this one trade can save all your losses.

But mind it; the hedge trade has to be squared in the end. This means you will never square up this trade in the middle of the day. Once you have squared up all your bullish trades, it will be squared up in the last. After making a basket, we will move on to Step 4.

STEP 4 - SECTORAL ANALYSIS

After making a basket of four trades (three bullish and one bearish), we will check which sectors are currently in high demand and which have high supply. We will choose three bullish stocks from the sectors in high demand and one bearish stock from a sector with high supply. Here, we will take help from the UDTS© Intraday Screener to save time and effort. You can use other ways also. For example, in UDTS© Intraday Screener – Sectoral Analysis, we can choose the top sectors in demand and those in supply.

Say we have chosen Banking and IT as the top-demanding sectors and FMCG as the high-supply sector.

After marking the bullish and bearish sectors, we will move to Step 5.

STEP 5 - STOCK SELECTION AS PER THE SIX PARAMETERS OF UDTS©

In this step, we will choose three bullish stocks from Banking or IT that is also bullish on six UDTS© parameters and one bearish stock from the FMCG sector that is also bearish on six UDTS© parameters. To save our time and effort, we will also take help from the UDTS© Intraday Screener to find bullish and bearish stocks on six UDTS© parameters.

Say we have chosen ICICI Bank, Infosys, and State Bank for bullish trades and HLL for bearish trades from the FMCG sector.

Now my basket is (+ ICICI Bank + Infosys + State Bank – HLL)

I will put the same amount in all four stocks in my intraday trading.

This trading model can give you the highest winning probabilities if you apply it correctly. I suggest all my students make paper trades on this trade model and make at least nine baskets for the next nine trading days. After that, you can self-judge the accuracy of this trading strategy. Along with the strategy, one should practice and gain experience to achieve full command in intraday trading.

Earning = Right Strategy + Practice + Experience

So, bye-bye to guesswork and gambling!!!

CHAPTER 20

WHY UDTS© BETTER THAN AI-BASED TRADING SOFTWARE?

Over the past decade, the belief that artificial intelligence could solve the complexities of the stock market has spread like wildfire. The notion is that humans lack the capacity and capability compared to machines, who will, without fail, consistently beat the market over time. By simply programming a machine, it will produce the ultimate formula, making you filthy rich in the process.

Unfortunately, though, this is a mere fantasy.

AI SOFTWARE IS FULLY DEPENDENT ON TECHNICAL ANALYSIS TOOLS

AI-based software utilities only respect the technical aspects and are based on technical tools that avoid any consideration of current news and data. Any veteran trader will tell you that the market isn't there to give away free money. Instead, it's a competitive environment that punishes anyone who tries to make a quick buck by trading on reactionary information already priced in.

UDTS© mechanism considers news and data as part of its strategy, which AI software utilities don't.

STOP-LOSSES ON SOFTWARE UTILITIES ARE PREDICTABLE

Normally, such software utilities have a standing instruction for stop-losses based on technical analysis tools, and once the price breaches support or resistance, it cuts the position automatically. These stop-loss points are normally manipulated by big traders and punters. They know that in intraday trading, the maximum stop-loss orders are inserted according to the technical tools. These punters know how much price to be taken temporarily up or down so that stop-losses of maximum people can be cut. And with one spike of price volatility, they show the exit doors to the general public using Algo and AI-based software utilities.

The UDTS©, on the other hand, has a special mechanism so that you cannot become the prey of big punters who cut the stop-loss at lower prices and, after that, take the price to new highs and leave the trader full of frustration.

AI SOFTWARE UTILITIES ARE TO MAKE BROKERAGES FOR BROKERS

Such software utilities provide more benefits to brokers than traders. They are built on the "Maximum Trades = Maximum Brokerage" strategy for brokers. Give your client 20 calls and get brokerage on 40 trades (20 buys + 20 sells).

Such software utilities are built on very minimum demand and supply parameters. Just one or two parameters are achieved. These software utilities send a buy or sell signal to the client. This way, you can get five to ten buy or sell signals daily.

The truth about the brokerage industry is that it makes money even when its clients lose. So when your broker offers you a plethora of trading algorithms to choose from, the alarm bells should be ringing.

Still, you may fall for the con because the trickery itself is seductive—let the algorithms do everything for you, so sit back and relax until you can retire. All the algorithm has to do is choose the right direction, i.e., either buy or sell, right? Wrong.

In reality, feeding an algorithm with purely technical data is the equivalent of putting a blindfold on an archer; he may hit the board one on ten times, but he'll miss nine out of ten times.

Whereas UDTS©, on the other hand, has six parameters, or we can say six filters. When a trade is passed by all the parameters or filters, only then it shows the maximum demand or supply point.

Due to these six filters, the strategy advocated quality trades over quantitative trades.

SOFTWARE UTILITIES DON'T HAVE EXPERIENCE AS HUMANS

AI is doomed to fail at stock market prediction. Beating the stock market over time, however, is possible. The solution lies with us because we, THE humans, have an edge called experience, which these software utilities lack. We have the ability to make informed decisions by analysing future catalysts of an asset and the reasons why they will move the price up or down.

CHAPTER 21
COMMON QUESTIONS IN THE MIND OF TRADERS/FAQS

If you're trading in the stock market, you've probably encountered at least one of these unsolved dilemmas at one point. Let's see if you can answer some of them now after understanding the right way to trade and clearing up any confusion:

1. When I sell, the market goes up
2. When I buy, the market goes down
3. I am fed up with the stock market; my luck is terrible in the stock market
4. When I trade, my profits are peanuts, but my losses are enormous
5. The index is rising and touching new highs, but my portfolio is always down

Does this sound like something you need help with? Let's take a closer look at each issue and try to resolve it.

1. WHEN I SELL, THE MARKET GOES UP.

It's a common phenomenon that the market goes up whenever the trader sells shares. And this happens most of the time because a trader receives only the momentary upsurge and fails to comprehend the trend. Despite being in a bullish trend, the profits are meagre, and the trader feels cheated by the market. So never sell in rising markets and wait until the trend starts downward momentum. Let's understand from a simple example: let's say you buy a share for ₹10 and then sell it when it reaches ₹12, netting a 20% profit. But due to the bullish trend, the prices keep soaring, and later, the trader feels that he must have sold it for ₹14 or even ₹16. Rather, a trader should only sell when the price starts downward momentum.

This means a clear understanding of the trend and the exact level of exit that needs to be included. Keep a note of this point because this is what we learned in the previous section of UDTS©.

2. WHEN I BUY, THE MARKET GOES DOWN.

This happens again when traders try to buy in falling markets. If the stock price falls from ₹100 to ₹95, then to ₹90, and ₹85, the trader may feel that the stock is now undervalued at ₹85. This could be a good opportunity to buy the stock in the hope that the price will eventually rebound. Of course, there is no guarantee that this will happen, and the trader may end up losing money because the stock is falling. Hence, a trader should not enter with a buy position until it takes a reversal trend.

The UDTS© strategy is a simple way for traders to create an exit and entry plan. This strategy involves looking at the current share price and then deciding to buy or sell based on whether the price is above or below a certain level.

3. I AM FED UP WITH THE STOCK MARKET; MY LUCK IS TERRIBLE IN THE STOCK MARKET.

If you trade without knowledge, you will always be in 95% of people who are losing and blaming their luck for that. Convert your lousy luck to good luck by following the right strategy, discipline, and knowledge.

4. WHENEVER I TRADE, MY PROFITS ARE PEANUTS, BUT MY LOSSES ARE ENORMOUS.

This is an exciting question. Even after learning proper strategies and advanced tools of technical analysis, a trader's portfolio is in the red, so what's wrong? Let's take an example to understand this: I bought a stock at ₹100; my target was ₹105, and my stop-loss was ₹97. However, once the stock started rising, I took a profit at ₹102 as my emotions overpowered my strategy, and I got a 2% profit. And in the same case, if the stock declines after I buy and comes to my stop-loss,

I could not exit at ₹97 as my emotions said, "Let's wait for some more time to shed 3%." And soon after that, the stock came to ₹93, and at last, I had to exit the trade at ₹93, paying a 7% loss.

In the above example, those traders who do not follow strategy, discipline, and rules make more losses than profits. That is why their profits are peanuts, but their losses are enormous.

5. LASTLY, A COMMON COMPLAINT: THE INDEX IS RISING AND TOUCHING NEW HIGHS, BUT MY PORTFOLIO IS ALWAYS DOWN.

This happens just for two reasons:

1. You have not selected the right stocks
2. You need the right timing of entry and exit from stocks

Here, I am talking about trading portfolios. People often think that a portfolio is made for long-term investing only. Still, my dear friend, ace traders also make proper portfolios when they trade. The motive to make the right trading portfolio is to keep your ledger always in green, no matter if the market is rising or falling. A trader should make a proper portfolio even if he is doing intraday trading. This way, by the end of the day, he can walk away, taking some money in his pocket for sure.

First, never trade in a single stock because no one can guarantee whether a single trade we bought or sold will give us a sure shot profit or not as we are not gambling, and our main motive is to bring home profits, whether less or more. To improve our probability of winning, we have to take a basket of at least 2-4 trades we have to keep in our basket so that if one stock does not go with my trend, another stock may cover that gap.

Also, note that a basket of stocks should have the right stocks. The stocks you buy should be in a rising trend, and those you sell should be in a downward trend.

Moreover, entering and exiting the stock also significantly affects your profits. If you enter and exit the stock at the right time, you can raise your profits and lessen your losses.

AUTHOR'S STORY

My 30-year journey can help young students who want to make their career in the stock market, amateur traders, professionals who want to work as sub-brokers, and people who are losing money in the stock market.

The journey will also help you understand what mistakes should be avoided.

It has been 30 years since being an amateur trader to becoming a mature trader, and I am still learning. I was a young amateur trader who needed more experience and understanding of the markets. I would make trades based on gut instinct and hope for the best. Thankfully, I have come a long way since then.

I have learned some essential lessons about life in the most brutal way. As a trader or an investor, you must take learnings back daily. Patience, constant learning, valuing time, and not being greedy are four virtues you must remember as a stock trader.

The stock market gives ample opportunity to earn but only to those who deserve it. So, here's a sneak peek at the professional journey that made me who I am today.

I owe all my success and fame to the Stock Market. My Best Teacher!!!

1. STOCK MARKET HAS BEEN MY DESTINY

The stock market has been my destiny, but not my choice. Regarding your career, there are ideal options to which every parent wants their child to stick. Unfortunately, the stock market doesn't even exist on this list. After completing high school and reaching the second year of graduation in 1992, it was clear I would not be a doctor or an engineer. After three attempts at N.D.A., that profession seemed out of reach too. So, there was new pressure on me to get a job; but I didn't know where or what to do. My father was going to retire in 1995, so my brother and I had to start earning. No one in my entire family or my friend circle knew even a thing about the stock market.

7 August 1992, the Harshad Mehta case tainted the stock market picture in everyone's mind. As a result, the stock market crashed by almost 72%. It was one of the biggest crashes in the Indian stock market's history.

Amidst all the turmoil, necessity brought me here. I got a job on little persuasion of acquaintances under a stockbroker in Delhi Stock Exchange RN Mittal and Company and later B.K. Jallan & Co.

My destiny changed from there. Not having an adequate skill set and qualification and a need for regular income ensured that I was glued to my job.

2. MY JOURNEY IN PRIMARY, AS WELL AS A SECONDARY MARKET TO RING TRADING

The crunch of staff forced me to take all the opportunities. I was lucky enough to experience ring trading. It's something only some people have had the chance to see, and it's an exciting and enjoyable experience. Ring trading is a unique form of trading conducted on a big pavilion by traders and jobbers appointed by member brokers of the exchange. It's a fast-paced and thrilling way to trade, and I'm glad I had the opportunity to participate. It was an experience of its kind, with many people in a vast room, shouting and bidding at the top of their voices; buying and selling stocks was all manual. At the end of the day, accounts were reconciled on Chaupadi (trade book), and I had to rush to clients to collect money for their purchases.

In the evening, after a busy day, many brokers and big traders would gather at the famous Broadway restaurant on Asif Ali Road near the

Delhi Stock Exchange. That was the informal joint where working days would be discussed over a glass of wine. It was all so filmy.

Many times I, too, joined them with my seniors. Though I was pretty young then, I got the opportunity to sit and hear the manoeuver of stock trading from the horse's mouth, which gave me learning at a very grass root level.

I learned a lot by just hearing stories on the stock market. I have also shared many such stories with you in this book. This definitely gave me exposure to the other side of the table, about the risks of a broker and client's behaviour.

3. WORKING IN THE RING WAS A DIFFERENT EXPERIENCE

Working in that crowd, booking the trade, and confirming with the clients—today, many people will need help understanding this essential exercise as there are online trading platforms that have changed the process a lot. Whoever has had experience in ring trading understands the fundamental nature of the market. I observed how traders were making and losing money. The trading was entirely manual—no digitalisation. In those days, we made strategies on the floor with thousands of traders beside us and saw them buying and selling stocks for their clients. It was very different from strategies made in A.C. chambers. Every day was a new experience for me in a never-before-seen world.

4. REALISATION OF ANALYTICAL SKILLS

In 1993, I had my college exams. I had to pass these exams to complete my graduation. I had stopped attending classes due to my full-time job, so attempting these exams was difficult. I devised a strategy to get through this too. I studied the past years' question papers and did a trend analysis. I did the calculations to figure out the bare minimum that I needed to study that could make me pass those exams. This was when I developed analytical skills. This necessitated sharpening my skill, which was dormant till that time. I never knew that this set of my abilities would get seasoned one day and lead to the making of Uni-Directional Trade Strategies, the universal way to trade in all markets.

5. MARKET TAUGHT ME THE ACTUAL MEANING OF DISCIPLINE.

Between 1993 and 1995, going through the ring trading experience developed a sense of discipline within me. The market used to open early in the morning, and you had to get there no matter what. It didn't matter if it was raining or if you were sick. The market didn't understand the crisis or situation in your personal life. This inculcated a sense of responsibility and discipline that nothing else could. The people who work in ring trading become robotic. This habit got inculcated within my blood, within my mind. By 1995, I was very disciplined. Due to this work ethic, new traders started working with me and believing in my work.

6. I LOST MY JOB, AND TRADING WAS MY ONLY LIVELIHOOD.

At the beginning of the year 1997, I lost my job. The broker with whom I was working had to shut down his company. I didn't know what to do as I didn't have any other skills. I couldn't start working in a new sector at this point. Trading was my bread and butter. So in the final quarter of 1997, I started as a sub-broker under Jain Capital Services. As a sub-broker, my only job was to bring in new accounts and earn brokerages. All the traders, clients, and friends, who believed in my strategies and ideology, joined me. They opened their trading accounts under my sub-broker ship. Now I also started earning additional income from my client's trades as a brokerage. This was an excellent decision taken by me after leaving my job. This way, along with my personal trading, I also started making money from the brokerage.

7. MANUAL TRADING TO ONLINE TRADING—THE GOLDEN PERIOD.

In 1999 and 2000, the world of stock trading changed dramatically. Ring trading—the norm for centuries—was replaced by online trading. This new system was faster, more efficient, and allowed greater transparency. While there were initially some teething problems, online trading quickly became the new norm, and ring trading disappeared.

The dematerialising of stocks began in the early 2000s when online trading took place. Today, everything is done electronically, and very little human intervention is involved. To stay in the market and succeed, I had to relearn how to trade online, which was a new world. The online world was much faster-paced, with much more information to process. I had to learn how to read the charts and make quick decisions. It was a challenge, but I'm glad I made the switch.

8. WHEN TRADERS STARTED BELIEVING MY IDEOLOGY

Many old traders joined me. My clients and I used to do intraday trading for our livelihoods. Between 1997 and 2000, I again received a lot of success. I had about 100-150 traders with me who believed in me. We earned a lot in the dot-com bubble till 2000.

9. THE DOT-COM BUBBLE INCIDENT WAS A BLOW TO MY CONFIDENCE AND LEARNING

The stock market is the best teacher, guide, and motivator if only one listens and obeys it like a good student. The stock market is a strict teacher of discipline, obedience, time management, and risk appetite. The market does not hear any excuses; you must pay for your miscalculations and inaccuracies. This happened to me also in March 2000.

The market taught me "Not to put all eggs in the same basket" during its four days of rigorous training.

In March 2000, when the dot-com bubble was nearly exploding, I was riding high on my career. I made good wealth by trading and broking in a small span of 5 years, from 1995 to 2000. But I was too overconfident in my achievements. Starting from a meagre salary of ₹2000 to accumulating ₹21 lakhs was too much for me. The money came quickly, and luck was always on my side, whether I was getting a job with a stock broker despite being an undergraduate or working as a sub-broker in 1997. I started to think I was experienced enough and knew all the market moves. But the market has its own way of handling overconfident traders.

IT stocks were on a boom in India from 1997 to 2000. There was the introduction of computers everywhere in the private and government sectors, and stocks in the IT sectors were selling like hotcakes. I remember trading very aggressively in the IT sectors and taking about 60 lacs positions in HFCL at 2500 and Pentamedia Graphics at 2800, which was earlier called Pentafour software.

I deposited my entire capital of ₹21 lakhs to my broker as security against my position. It was a good security amount, almost one-third of the total value.

In March 2020, the IT meltdown began. As soon as the news about the overvaluation of these stocks poured in, the stock prices nosedived. This was because the stocks were overvalued five to six times. As a result, a stock of ₹400 was selling at over ₹2500. That was Friday, the last trading day of the week when the community was informed about the overvaluation of stocks and losses incurred by the IT giants.

HFCL and Penta Software were also on that list. The realisation of the biggest mistake of my life began. **I had invested my entire capital in just two companies in the same sector.**

The following Saturdays and Sundays were the densest and most anxious days of my life. I eagerly waited for the Monday market to open, praying for a miracle.

I decided to exit my position on Monday and decided to book the losses on the very first day. I reached my office well before 9 a.m. and was all geared up to square off, but to my jitters, both the stocks froze in lower circuits below 10%, and trading was halted for the day. I lost ₹6 lakhs on my ₹60 lakh position and got no chance to exit. The broker was after me to submit ₹6 lakhs immediately. With all my persuasion, I convinced the broker that I would square off the position as soon as the freeze opened. Unfortunately, the freeze didn't open on Monday. The entire day was lost, and I had to carry my position for the next day. On Tuesday, again, both stocks froze at a lower circuit of 10% within a fraction of a second of opening the market.

Almost 20% (i.e., about ₹12 lakh) was wiped from my total capital of ₹21 lakhs. However, there was no chance or hope, as my position was still in the market. Following Wednesday, the same thing repeatedly happened—both of my stocks froze again below 10% of the circuit breaker. At this time, HFCL came around 1900, and Penta Software came around 2100, denting my account by almost 30% loss in just three trading sessions.

On Thursday, the market opened, and again, it was near the circuit breaker. I got a chance of hardly a minute to throw away my positions. At last, I sold my entire position at almost 35% losses, taking losses of ₹22-23 lakh back home. I lost my real hopes, dreams, and money in just four days. I never want to recall those days of my career.

These four days taught me an unforgivable, lifelong lesson for trading and investing. But, unfortunately, this lesson cost me ₹21 lakhs for four days of rigorous learning.

Today, I narrate this incident to all my students, so they don't fall prey to this market. I always insist on learning. We never had a school to learn about the stock market. The stock market was and is my most excellent teacher.

Despite the losses, I didn't leave the stock market because I was not very qualified and had given time and effort to the stock market; quitting was never an option for me.

10. GATHERED COURAGE AND SHARPENED LEARNINGS TO BE A PRUDENT TRADER

In 2001, my parents arranged my marriage. I discussed the losses with my would-be wife, who wisely advised me to take them as a part of learning and asked me to swear never to repeat this mistake. Losses suffered in 2000 made me very, very conservative. I had no other option to venture into. The stock market was where I belonged. Now I had to define myself. Was I a trader? Was I a sub-broker?

I started upgrading myself and studying various NSE modules to sharpen my knowledge and skills, and I attempted the exams at NSE. I also started attending NSE workshops. The journey till 2008 was very enriching in terms of knowledge and experience.

I started working more intensely on the sub-broker ship. During this time, online platforms started booming in India. I took one more online sub-broker ship of Reliance securities ltd. I partnered with the pioneer of online trading in India. Due to this, I was able to connect 5000 traders with me. Online trading had become a buzzword by then. Things were going well till 2008.

I also started informal education sessions with my clients on Saturdays. It was more of a knowledge and experience exchange session.

11. MY EMOTIONAL OUTBURST.

In 2008, the Subprime/Lehman Brothers crisis shook the markets globally. The tsunami was intense, and its effects were seen in Indian markets too. The NSE crashed by almost 70% in just nine months. This time, the clients connected to me suffered more losses than I did. It affected my clients, friends, and everyone who believed in me. This was an emotional setback for me. I thought the things I taught them didn't work for them, and they suffered from this loss due to me. This brought a sense of guilt and self-doubt within me. I decided that I would quit the stock market now. I decided to put a stop to my career of 16 years.

However, my wife strongly objected to the career change because the risk was too high with kids and my ageing parents. She made me realise that the discipline I had taught my clients and traders needed to be better grasped. If they had understood well, they wouldn't have suffered the losses. Finally, I realised it was true.

I decided to teach my clients better. So I went out of my way to conduct classes for my clients on weekends in my office. This was a milestone. It gave a new direction to my journey.

12. AS A MENTOR.

Till 2013, I casually taught my clients on weekends. I, too, learned a lot of new things in this process. We turned Saturdays into revision days. First, we used to analyse our decisions and mistakes. Then, we started learning from our mistakes. Finally, we began realising errors that we could have avoided. These sessions on Saturdays turned into fun sessions where we hung out and had constructive discussions.

13. STARTED FORMAL EDUCATION FOR TRADERS.

In 2013, I formally entered stock market education. I started a workshop called 'My Way of Trading: Art of Trading.' I started teaching my students about intraday trading. Even though it is one of the challenging professions, it attracts the most common people. They believe they can earn within 2-3 hours. However, these 2-3 hours could take away your money too. For intraday trading, people just need to know the market trend and what steps they need to take. It was not a gamble. It was just a deeper understanding of demand and supply. Teaching my clients a more profound understanding of demand and supply in a simple way was a challenge in itself. But my everyday teaching experience between 2008 and 2013 started improving, and it ultimately helped me. Slowly, more and more people began understanding intraday trading and started earning from it. This rejuvenated the confidence within me.

14. THE MAKING OF UDTS©

One thing that kept bothering me was that most students with knowledge of 25-30 technical tools still needed to improve while trading. The problem was choosing the right tool to apply in different market conditions.

These workshops eventually gave birth to the UDTS© strategy in 2018. I call this strategy the sum of my experience in the stock market. This strategy explains the basic chart of demand and supply that will eventually help you make decisions and analyse trends regarding intraday trading. The launch of this strategy was very random. YouTube had just started gaining momentum in 2018. So, one day, we just recorded an art of trading exercise from our mobile camera and uploaded it on YouTube. This video went viral and gained over 10 million views.

15. ON VIEWER'S DEMAND

With my team of faculties, we designed a trading strategy that was more practically oriented and almost like a step-by-step way to move in the market that would work in all difficulties and price movements. There was a need for a proper strategy. This included adequate risk management, diversification, understanding market conditions, and all other parameters that can raise the winning probability of a trader.

UDTS© BECAME THE BEST ONLINE SELLING COURSE IN INDIA

In 2018 when the UDTS© was launched, it became a tool for common people. It didn't have any cumbersome tools, but it was based on basic charts. As a result, it has the greatest potential for returns.

I have learned from my losses and profits that there is no one-size-fits-all approach to entering the market. Every situation is different, and every need is another. The best way to learn is to take your losses and profits as they come and learn from them by asking yourselves why this profit has come to you or why this loss occurred. So, keep asking yourselves these small questions. You will definitely get all the answers from this market itself.

I have mentored 10,000 students across all genders, ages, and ethnicity. The journey till now has been satisfying. I pray to the Almighty to bestow me with all the strength and wisdom I need to continue my journey in the stock market. The online sessions, webinars, seminars, and workshops have also benefited me. In my weekly Episode of T.A.S.K. Based on UDTS© and M.A.D.E©, I share my analysis and learnings of the previous week and give levels of NIFTY and Bank NIFTY, which are always accurate.

Happy Learning!!

Happy Trading!!

WHY DO I LIKE THIS PROFESSION?

The stock market attracts one and all. In my story, I did mention that quitting the stock market was never an option for me. I developed a love for the market, despite its unpredictability. The versatility of the stock market made my love of the market deeper and deeper.

I am sharing some of the best attributes of this market with you all:

1. **It is easy money:** It looks like a lucrative option for earning money quickly. You put in some money and gain a lot of it back. New technological advances have turned everything online, thus making it easier.
2. **You are your own boss:** You don't have to work under a tyrant boss following orders. You make your own decisions.
3. **It is a skilled profession:** It involves learning strategies and technical tools. You can further apply these skill sets to a job in finance.
4. **Good work-life balance:** The stock market opens at 9 a.m. and closes at 3:30 p.m. I have all the time for my family after that. I get Saturdays and Sundays off to focus on my personal life.
5. **No raw material, no labour, no warehouse:** It doesn't require you to set up a space or a factory. You don't have to hire workers. You don't have to spend energy either for managing an office and your workers.
6. **White collar business/job.** You don't have to put in any physical effort. You just have to use your brain energy in the 6-7 hours you work.

FOLKLORE OF GREED AND FEAR IN THE TRADING COMMUNITY THE GREEDY GHANSHYAM

Once, two friends, Shyam and Ghanshyam, were walking along a river.

Ghanshyam saw a blanket flowing in the river. He asked Shyam to go and grab the blanket. Shyam warned him not to be greedy, as the river flow was very fast, and they could die.

But Ghanshyam was adamant and jumped into the river to bring the blanket. He ran across, and just as he put his hand on the blanket, the blanket caught him, and he fiercely feared and started screaming for help.

Shyam, across the bank, asked him not to be greedy and urged him to leave the blanket and return. Ghanshyam shouted, ""मैं तो छोड़ दूँ लेकिन यह कंबल मुझे नहीं छोड़ता," meaning, "I am ready to let go of this blanket, but this blanket is not letting me go."

What Ghanshyam presumed to be a blanket was actually a bear. Ghanshyam lost his life due to greed.

Moral: Don't be greedy in the market. The market does not spare the greedy.

The story and characters are imaginary; it is as narrated by my senior colleagues on ring trading day

This story is the true depiction of greed and fear of the market. People often fall prey to it unknowingly. When people come to trade without knowledge and proper strategy, they often lose money.

UDTS© aims to keep greed and fear under control and helps traders to take the best decision for themselves.

Learning never stops at IFMC®. Keep learning and keep upgrading with us.

Do share your feedback with us on info@ifmcinstitute.com